Stories in Stone

Stories in Stone

The Sdok Kok Thom Inscription & the Enigma of Khmer History

John Burgess

First published and distributed in 2010 by River Books
396 Maharaj Road, Tatien, Bangkok 10200
Tel. 66 2 222-1290, 225-0139, 224-6686
Fax. 66 2 225-3861
E-mail: order@riverbooksbk.com
www.riverbooksbk.com

Copyright collective work © River Books, 2010
Copyright text © John Burgess
Copyright photographs © John Burgess,
except where otherwise indicated.

All rights reserved. No part of this book may be reproduced or transmitted in any form or by any means, electronic or including photocopy, recording or any other information storage and retrieval system, without prior permission in writing from the publisher.

Publisher: Narisa Chakrabongse
Editor: Stephen A. Murphy
Production supervision: Paisarn Piemmattawat
Design: Reutairat Nanta

ISBN 978 616 7339 01 6

Printed and bound in Thailand
by Sirivatana Interprint Public Co., Ltd.

Front cover: *View of the inner eastern* gopura *of Sdok Kok Thom in 1979.*
Frontispiece: *The Sdok Kok Thom inscription. Courtesy of RBC.*
Back cover: *Camp 007 Khmer Serei militia leader In Sakhan (left),*
    circa *1979. Courtesy of Timothy Carney.*

Contents

Acknowledgments	6
The Exodus	8
The Priest	16
An Empire Built and Lost	24
The Naturalist	30
The Linguist	36
Mission to Sdok Kok Thom	46
Messages from the Past	52
Sadashiva's Testament	60
The Great Conqueror	64
The God King	72
Dates Confused	80
The Brahmin Landlords	90
The Resident Spirit	96
Pillage	100
The Stone's Fate	106
Resistance Stronghold	112
Lethal Souvenirs	122
Restoration	128
Holy Ground Contested	134
The Temple Today	142
Why Sadashiva Wrote	150
Postscript	156
The Sdok Kok Thom Inscription: Full Translation	160
Glossary	192
Further Reading	196

Acknowledgments

Many people helped birth this book. Foremost is my wife Karen, who shared the tumult of the Khmer refugee exodus with me in 1979 and in more recent times encouraged my writing plans, critiqued content and structure and sent me off on lengthy research trips. My daughter Katharine helped with research in London, while my daughter Sarah helped with French language. Both added enthusiasm for the project as well as feedback on the manuscript. I thank my mother Alice Burgess, who by taking me to Angkor in 1969 got me started on a life-long fascination with Khmer antiquity. And I thank my late father David Burgess, whose work in and love for Asia brought our family to Thailand in 1966.

Other people lent specific knowledge and resources. Chhany Sak-Humphry produced the sharp and euphonious translation that was my first real introduction to the inscription. She graciously agreed to let my book include a revised full text of the translation that she did with assistance from Philip N. Jenner. Bernard and Lieselotte Kessler generously shared personal letters, photos and the unpublished memoir of Bernard's great uncle Étienne Aymonier, as well as putting up me and daughter Sarah at their remarkable home, a moated medieval castle that they lovingly restored with their own hands. Architect Vasu Poshyanandana gave me hours of his time to recount the challenges of the temple's modern reconstruction. Khmer history scholars Im Sokrithy and Ang Choulean helped guide me to good information and away from bad. Sos Kem and Sophal Mony gave me contacts and insights into Khmer culture. Timothy Carney read the manuscript and offered suggestions based on his long experience with Cambodia and its history.

Thanawat Samrankit and Nipon Prompilai, English teachers at the Tupprayapittaya School near the temple, introduced me to people in the community and interpreted in interviews, and Nipon shared his own childhood encounter with a left-over bomb. Sompong and Sitthipong Prompilai (Nipon's parents), the late Kancharup Champasook, Somsak Leesirisakul, Leung Gert-thong and Saguan Savangcheung told me of the temple's role in the local community in the first half of the 20th century. William Mour Ley, Sokry Sum, Cameron Macauley, Gaffar Peang-Meth and Hang Sobratsavyouth recounted refugee-period memories of the temple. Apichat Tawepoka, author of a Thai-language book which bears the English title *The Sdok Kok Thom Code*, generously shared historical findings and photographs. Johan Van Zyl gave a detailed account of his year of work to remove munitions from the temple area.

M.L. Pattaratorn Chirapravati kindly provided a photograph of the inscription stone. Sran Thongpan and Suthikiet Sopanik found other photos for me. Nga Hillenbrand, Thérèse Arcole and Delphine Schrank helped with difficult French language tasks, including deciphering Aymonier's sometimes mystifying 19th century handwriting. Luang Poh Suwan Kanthathamo welcomed me into his monastery next to Sdok Kok Thom and Phrakru Wapee Sangkhakit told me of modern-day religious life in the area. Other assistance came from Vornida Seng, Daniel Michon, Kelvin So, Hay S. Meas, Pierre Singaravelou, Vichien Charernporn, Peter Sharrock, Tomasina Galiza, Michael Abrams, Asger Mollerup and Tamar Gabelnick.

Helping me locate books, documents and articles were staff members at the Thai National Library, the Siam Society Library, the Asian Institute of Technology Library, the Damrong Rajanubhab Library, the British Library, the Library of the School of Oriental and African Studies, the Bibliothèque nationale de France, the École française d'Extrême-Orient libraries in Paris (special thanks to Isabelle Poujol there), Bangkok and Siem Reap, the Cambodian National Library, the Library of Congress, the Princeton University Library and the *Bangkok Post* newspaper.

I, of course, also thank the Internet, which in a few seconds delivered free of charge resources that otherwise would have cost me heavily in time and money. Among them were satellite photos of Sdok Kok Thom, the complete text of Aymonier's *Le Cambodge* and Thai students' accounts of weekend outings to the temple.

Finally, I thank the priest Sadashiva, whose stories and temple enabled me to taste of life a thousand years ago in one of the world's greatest civilisations. I hope that this book will allow others to do the same.

John Burgess

The monuments of Cambodia speak not only through their style and their sculpture. They are full of inscriptions traced on door frames, on free-standing stones placed in interiors or close to sanctuaries.

Étienne Aymonier,
linguist and archaeologist, 1902

Sdok Kok Thom main sanctuary, from the west, 1979.

Chapter I – The Exodus

Sometime in the middle of 1979 – no one agrees exactly when – a city was born in dry forest land along the border of Cambodia and Thailand. It was a city of refugees. The Khmer Rouge had been recently overthrown, and Cambodians fortunate enough to be alive were free to pick up and go where they wanted. Many chose to make for a frontier settlement that became known as Camp 007. Flies, thieves, dysentery, huts roofed with blue plastic sheeting – these were the sad realities of life at 007. But people continued to come, day after day, on foot, on bicycles with patched tires, on carts drawn by pairs of bony oxen. In the Cambodian interior, they faced war and famine; here on the border was a ration of hope. Here people might buy food with gold jewellery dug up from village hiding places. They might sleep off malaria chills, look for lost family members or simply live for a time free of the dictates of some stern political movement. At its peak, the camp's population totalled perhaps one hundred thousand.

Foreign journalists soon found their way to the place, walking in along rice paddy dikes from a Thai road that passed a kilometre away. I was one of them, a young freelancer trying to make his way in the profession. Everyone I met in the camp had a story in turn heartbreaking, horrifying and inspiring – friends lost to a Khmer Rouge execution squad; trips into the jungle to forage for food; a husband so sick he had to be left behind. Telling these things to a perspiring foreigner with a notebook, it seemed, could have the same purging effect as testifying in the witness stand of a truth and reconciliation commission.

Taking down the accounts could be exhausting work. The flies and the heat, the armed men who hovered around (they were the self-appointed local authorities) didn't make it any easier. Sometimes I needed a break. So I would close the notebook, say thanks and go for a walk.

One day, I turned down a trail into some forest land, curious to see if any new huts had sprung up there – the camp was in constant flux. But there were none this day, no sign of people at all, in fact. Soon I found myself in some welcome solitude, shade and cool. I wandered on for a bit. Then, ahead – something strange, half-hidden in the foliage. Silent, solid, permanent, everything the settlement somewhere off behind me was not. After a few more steps I could see that the something was a ruined temple. It lay in the embrace of tropical vines and trees, unresisting. Many of

Trees and stonework at Sdok Kok Thom, 1979.

its stones had fallen to the ground. It seemed overall a mystical melding of nature and bygone human creativity.

I knew right away I was looking at a relic of the Khmer Empire, founded in 802 AD. A Hindu and later a Buddhist civilisation, it was possessed of one of history's greatest urges to build. Temples, palaces, bridges, stone-paved avenues, gates guarded by rows of carved gods, holy reservoirs running eight kilometres long – the word 'grandeur' was practically created with the Khmer Empire in mind. From its capital, Angkor, home to as many as a million people at its 12th century peak, political power projected outward for many hundreds of kilometres, tying together lands that today belong to Cambodia, Laos, Vietnam and Thailand. It is hard to overstate the historical import in the region. Angkor is to Southeast Asia as Rome is to Europe, great imperial forebear that continues in modern times to influence language, government, religion, literature and war.

I remember a quickened pulse, a disbelieving smile, a field of vision that seemed to narrow. I hurried forward.

Of course I was not the first to find this place. People of the district's old villages knew of it, as did many of the refugees, not to mention historians. But when I passed through its vine-draped gate, I saw no sign that anyone but me had come calling since its abandonment to the wilds centuries earlier. It felt like discovery.

I spent quite a bit of time that day and later ones playing amateur archaeologist, tramping over fallen stones, peering into mysterious holes. I had to step carefully – there were quite a few places for snakes to hide. The foliage was so thick it was hard to get a good view of the place. But slowly I figured out lay-out and scale. To the east, a dried-up rectangular holy reservoir about 350 metres long, linked to the temple by a ceremonial avenue on which weeds pressed up between the paving stones. A grand outer gate, giving entry though a perimeter wall that measured about 130 metres square. Then an inner gate and a collapsed central courtyard with sides that had once been a gallery of columns. A pair of smallish rectangular buildings of a type that scholars call libraries. At the courtyard's centre, the main sanctuary – most of its stones were missing, leaving a spindly pinnacle about ten metres high that somehow refused to submit to gravity. Perhaps that improbable feat helped me begin to sense spiritual significance as well. The goal of the empire's architects was to build heaven on earth, places of such aesthetic and geometric perfection that gods of the Hindu cosmos would descend to take up residence. This was such a place. Some of those gods were there as carvings: Vishnu asleep beneath the primordial sea, dreaming the next world into existence; holy

Northeastern library, Sdok Kok Thom,
photographed from the southwest, 1979.

elephants; a *naga*, benevolent serpent of Khmer mythology, holding its seven heads high.

By the time I came along, this place was a thousand years into its existence. I worried how much longer it could endure. No one was maintaining the temple; aggressive vines and tree roots continued to split its stones. Moreover, this part of the border periodically became a battlefield, with grenades and mortar shells exploding indiscriminately. But perhaps the most serious danger was theft. The private collectors of New York and Tokyo had long paid dearly for Khmer sculpture brought surreptitiously their way; there was now general lawlessness in the district and plenty of people needing money. I recall one day leaning down to inspect a fallen *naga* head and wondering just how long it would remain where it was.

Sometimes it felt wrong to be so engaged with a bygone place when there was present-day desperation on a mass scale five minutes away. But I kept coming, exploring that inner courtyard again, walking that processional avenue with the weeds pressing up between the stones. I began privately thinking of the temple as mine. Proprietary feelings were helped along by the fact that it was almost always deserted. The camp's people had plenty else to worry about and in any case their religious traditions held that worship is best conducted in a new place – the camp was dotted with makeshift Buddhist shrines – and that the strange spirits of an ancient Hindu site might not welcome their visits.

Still, it seemed fitting that the refugees had settled in so close by. I had arrived at their camp that first day thinking I was covering a new phase of a war that began in Cambodia in 1970, as a spill over from Vietnam. But the temple offered silent suggestion that the exodus was part of a process much larger and older. The human outflow was the latest chapter in the history of the Khmer Empire. Textbooks often say that the Siamese capture of Angkor in 1431 AD brought the empire to an end. But in fact it never really went away. The temples were abandoned, yes, but the state that built them merely shrank, eventually becoming Cambodia. The people in the camp were in effect present-day citizens of the empire. Certainly they had the same dignified square faces of the men and women of Angkor's bas reliefs. They drove wooden ox carts of the same design and lived by the same conviction that the world is a place ruled by spirits. And certainly they held the ancient glories close to their hearts. Angkor was and is the starting point of Cambodian national pride and notions of place in the world.

I returned to the United States in 1980. The Cambodian war continued. In 1984, the Vietnamese army destroyed the camp near

The Exodus

Sdok Kok Thom main sanctuary,
photographed from the east, 1979.

the temple. The refugees fled. In the 1990s peace slowly set in. The United Nations oversaw a ceasefire and elections. I kept up with news from the country and with a family I had first met in the camp. Cambodia reopened to the world and in 2002, my wife Karen and I took our two daughters to Angkor. We marvelled at what we saw. Back home, I began to read seriously into Khmer history, buying out-of-print books on the Internet.

In various studies, I came across references to a great bilingual inscription. Engraved with Sanskrit and the Old Khmer that was the common language of ancient Khmers, this metre and half-tall monolith was the starting point for any effort to understand the empire's history. Its roughly 340 lines offered a remarkable narrative covering precisely two hundred fifty years. There was no other Khmer inscription remotely like it.

A footnote said it was found at Prasat Sdok Kok Thom – Temple of the Great Reed Lake[1] – located on the Thai-Cambodian border.

It took a while, but then came revelation: Sdok Kok Thom was *my temple*.

I got my hands on a translation of the inscription.

To me, the only way in which Khmer ruins disappoint is that everybody who helped create them is long dead. I have always wondered what it would be like to flip the lever of a time machine and sit down with someone who lived in those times. Reading the inscription was the next best thing. An 11th century Hindu priest was speaking in verse across the ages, telling of things big and small – the conqueror prince who founded the empire, the spittoon that was partial payment for a tract of land, the repeated relocation of the capital. The position of planets in the heavens, a curse against thieves, the amassing of land by the priest's family – they were all there too. And a paean to the temple itself:

Whoso views this ideal abode, foremost on earth,
Or merely hears it spoken of,
His mind is at rest, his soul is sanctified.

But the testament gave rise to many questions as well. Why did the priest write with length and detail at odds with centuries of practice? Why was a text so rich in royal history left not in the capital but at what was, despite the priest's description, a

---

[1] The French generally romanised the name as Sdok Kak Thom. It is also rendered sometimes as Sadok Kok Thom. I am using Sdok Kok Thom, the most common form in English-language writing about the temple.

Vishnu sleeping in the Ocean of Creation, Sdok Kok Thom, 2009.

comparatively small provincial outpost of the empire? Which of his words recounted historical fact and which turned a blind eye to it so as to honour the religious and political ideals of the times?

I began to wonder what had happened to the temple in the quarter century since I had seen it. Was that *naga* somehow still there?

So I decided to go back, and to write this book. Certainly the time seemed right. With more than a million foreigners visiting each year, Angkor was finally starting to assume its due place in the world's consciousness alongside such fonts of civilisation as Rome, Xian and Machu Pichu. The Sdok Kok Thom inscription likewise deserves an honoured place with its peers – it's not too much to say that they include the Rosetta Stone and the Code of Hammurabi. It is my hope that this book will help accomplish that, by telling the tale of how so much of what we know about a great ancient empire comes from one stone and one priest's determination that stories not be lost.

Outer eastern *gopura*, Sdok Kok Thom, looking in, 2009.

Chapter II – The Priest

It is late on a wet season afternoon in the year 1052 AD. No weeds sprout in the processional avenue of Sdok Kok Thom. All have been plucked by villagers who tend the temple in shifts that last a waxing or a waning moon. No broken stones litter the central courtyard. Each is whole and in the place that heaven and its earthly architects intended. The many pieces are united as one, a tower that rises thirty cubits high, curving gently like a closed lotus blossom. Carved *naga* serpents and the bird god Garuda gaze down from its heights. Inside its single chamber is the focus of the temple's energies, the *linga*, a stone shaft in which resides the essence of the god Shiva.

The lord of this seat of worship is a man named Sadashiva, a Brahmin, member of Hinduism's priestly elite. His name, appropriately, means 'abiding in Shiva' in the Sanskrit language of the faith. Right now he is nowhere to be seen. But his retainers are passing the word that he is in his teak house just beyond the temple's outer wall, sequestered with his scribe, who has brought many stacks of the dried palm leaf strips on which records are kept. It seems that Sadashiva has some very big job to begin. It is weighing on him, everyone can sense.

He is the current patriarch of a family that for generations has led the Hindu spiritual life of this district. As a Brahmin, he is trusted of heaven, possessor of its secrets, incantations and magic. In religious processions, he sometimes rides in a hammock suspended on poles that his disciples shoulder. He wears a white garment tied about the waist. He has let his whiskers grow, his hair is knotted in a bun atop his head. Like everyone, he wears no shoes and leaves his chest bare, save for jewellery.

The Brahmin has in recent days returned from another trip to the capital, which lies about four days' travel to the east. He had close relations with the monarch who died two years earlier after a reign of nearly forty years and people have been watching for signs that his ties with the new king, Udayadityavarman, are equally close. Most people at the temple are now breathing easy on that question: the master was wed to the younger sister of the queen during one of his recent capital visits and received a new honorary name, Jayarendravarman, 'Conqueror-Indra-Protector,' which gives formal association with the thunder god Indra. But there are a few in the household who want to know why, if everything is going so well, the priest seems so burdened.

You would be that way too, the sceptics are told, if you'd passed the last five years the way the master has. He's been on the road all the time, barely ever resting, seeing to the rebuilding of temples and settlements that fell victim to the civil war. He has travelled back and forth to the capital too many times to count, going whenever His Majesty calls. He's always busy there, conducting rites and dealing with the royal land staff to add to the family's holdings. And of course he's had the tremendous responsibility of overseeing construction of our own new temple.

Sadashiva remains in his house, sending subordinate priests to carry out the daily rites at the temple's *linga*. Finally, word spreads that the master is drafting the temple's inscription. Of course, people say. The priest will need to mark for the ages the family's devotion to Shiva, the beneficence of the king in providing pitchers and gems and other religious fittings, and the precise date on which the *linga* was consecrated.

Day after day, the priest keeps out of sight. A new supply of writing chalk is taken into his chamber. Why are things taking so long? the retainers ask. The master's scribe, a man with fine hand writing and a flare for Sanskrit allusion, continues to spend hours with him. In the evenings, the man politely turns aside efforts by other members of the priestly household to pry things out of him.

Eight weeks after it began, the job is done. Everyone knows this because one morning a great collection of palm strips, bound together, leaves the abbot's house in the hands of a messenger who is bound for the capital with two bodyguards. The master, standing at the doorway, watches the departure.

Some weeks pass. The messenger returns from the capital, again carrying palm strips. Cloistered again in his house, the priest is seen reading them carefully. With the scribe back at his side, he is said to be making changes and additions. Then that job is finished too.

Several days later, an oxcart arrives from a quarry that provided much of the sandstone for the temple. The cart is bearing a particularly heavy load, a four-sided monolith as tall as a man. Half a dozen labourers ease it off the cart. A makeshift straw hut is erected around it, so that no one can see. A stonecutter arrives and all day long people hear the sound of chisel biting into stone. The inscription's words are taking their eternal form. Sometimes the priest is right there, looking over the man's shoulder as he works, sometimes adding to the text as he goes along. I would not want to be that stone cutter, people say.

Finally, this job too is done. But still, no one is allowed to see the monolith. It is covered over to await its official raising at a sheltered spot being prepared for it. It will stand at the temple courtyard's northeast corner, sheltered, in the space where the northern and eastern galleries intersect.

There is no record of Sadashiva sequestering himself during the wet season of 1052, nor of whispering among the temple's attendants. What you have read above is informed supposition as I try to reconstruct how one of the world's most remarkable testaments came to be created. At the same time I have tried to be true to the best historical and archaeological understanding of details of the temple, its implements, staff and daily routines.

On what basis, for instance, can it be said that Sadashiva was carried in a hammock suspended from poles? In the great Angkor Wat temple, a bas relief carved about a century after his time shows a chief Brahmin carried in such a conveyance. Thus it seems a good bet that a high-ranking priest such as Sadashiva was at times honoured in this way too. Likewise, I am safe in saying that his house was made of wood because not a single residence, whether for beggar or king, has survived from the Angkorian age. From this can be deduced that houses were of wood (the poor would have used bamboo), which doesn't last long in Southeast Asia's humid climate. In any case, we can see some of those houses and palaces in bas reliefs on temple walls in Angkor.

This kind of deduction is the stock in trade of Angkor scholars – the placing of one clue alongside a second and comparing them together with a third to draw some conclusion that will go on to become part of the accepted record for evaluating other evidence. There is no other way, because the historical record is thin. Broadly described, it consists of archaeological evidence, a few Chinese annals, sculpture and bas reliefs and a single eye-witness account, written by a Chinese envoy who arrived on a ship in the year 1296. And inscriptions. Most are short, many are parochial and not entirely legible, due to physical damage over the centuries. The general paucity of solid fact is one reason why the Sdok Kok Thom inscription stands out so prominently – more than 340 lines in one place, almost every word legible, a true cornucopia of informational offerings to historians.

Still, the inscription too is subject to endless deduction, beginning with questions of authorship. Sadashiva did not sign the inscription. But it names him repeatedly as head of the clan, and unlike many other people who are mentioned, he is not noted as having died. The text contains myriad points that could have been known only by him and the family, and that information is invariably presented in ways that cast a good light on his clan. Most historians take it as fact that he was the author. Chhany Sak-Humphry, one of the latest translators, has a more nuanced view. She suggests that the text was not meant to be taken as words from Sadashiva's mouth – the fulsome praise it bestows on him would violate the age's notions of priestly humility. She thinks it was intended as the words of the king. It would carry supreme authority that way. But in her view, Sadashiva could only have been busy behind the scenes, assisting a palace council in drafting it and approving the final version. Sak-Humphry's explanation seems the most logical to me, so I have depicted the priest sending off to the capital a large collection of written material, possibly including a word-for-word draft, then looking at the edited version that returns and committing it (with some final changes) to stone. Just as the words of a great speech really belong to the speech writer, I will treat the text as Sadashiva's composition.

With inscription written and carved, the priest rises early the next day to survey his realm before prayers at the *linga*.

Plans for the temple were drafted by a Brahmin architect who came out from the capital. But as with the inscription, Sadashiva

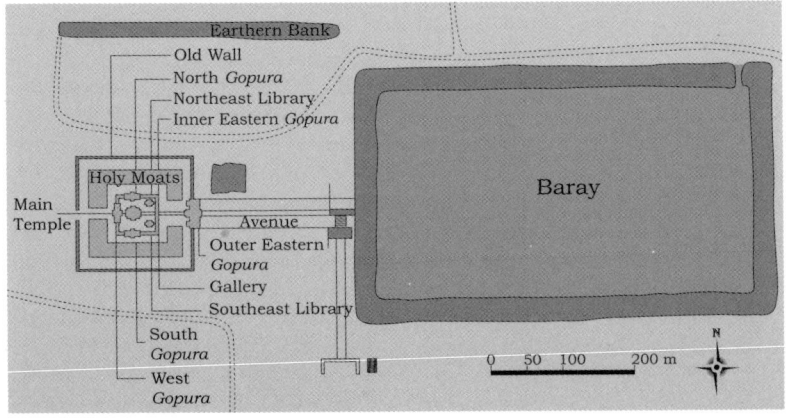

Map of Sdok Kok Thom as of 2009.

had extensive input on something so important to his family's standing on earth and in heaven. The temple that resulted could well be considered his own design – he knows it by its Sanskrit name, Bhadraniketana, Blessed Edifice of Worship.

To the east of the temple is its holy reservoir, its *baray*. Sadashiva now stands at the centre of its western edge. Defined by earthen dikes, it has a precise orientation to the four cardinal directions, as heavenly rules provide. From its northeast corner extends a levee that captures waters that collect naturally beyond the *baray* and channels them through a gap in the dikes. The water is at its annual high point just now, because it's wet season, about as deep as a man is tall.

The *baray* is a pleasure to gaze upon, as Sadashiva does now. The water is home to swans and many types of freshwater fish that find their way in through the stream. Residents of the local communities sometimes bring their nets and traps here, after asking permission of priest and gods. Yet the reservoir is also something of the divine realm. It is the Sea of Creation, the waters that ring the home of the Hindu gods, Mount Meru. To the depths of this sea the god Vishnu descends periodically. He slumbers on the floor, supported by the serpent Ananta, and dreams a new world into existence. From his navel is born the god Brahma, who continues the job of renewing the cycle of creation.

Behind Sadashiva is an avenue paved in the reddish clay-rock laterite. It leads west, toward the temple's outer *gopura*, or gate. Now he turns and walks this avenue, as he has since his priestly apprenticeship as a boy. He passes carved stone posts that line both sides. Off to the north a bit is an ashram, where acolytes live lives of prayer and service. The younger of them pitch in with temple maintenance duty, working in inner sanctums that are too holy for ordinary villagers to enter.

The outer *gopura* is the first hint of the splendours that lie within. Its sandstone, finely carved and cut, is almost white as bone, as the stone is when it is cut fresh from the quarry, but it contains hints of red and brown, even orange. Carved deities adorn the *gopura's* facade. This gate is a collection of true doors that people can pass through and false windows that only gods can. To the left and the right extend laterite walls that form the temple's outer perimeter defining a zone of holiness. Now Sadashiva climbs three laterite steps – by heaven's command, there must be only an odd number in a temple like this – and enters the slight gloominess of the *gopura's* interior. He passes minor shrines to his left and right.

Pediment of Sdok Kok Thom's northeastern library seen from the side, 1959. Courtesy of L'École française d'Extrême-Orient.

On the other side, down three steps, the avenue continues. On either side now are holy moats that are an extension of the Sea of Creation. Ahead is the inner *gopura*. It has a tower that curves like a lotus blossom, another preview of what lies inside. Sadashiva climbs again, this time five steps. He emerges into the inner courtyard, formed by four galleries. To his right and left are two stone buildings, their pediments alive with deities and floral patterns. But the focus of this paved courtyard lies directly ahead. It is the central sanctuary. It's another lotus tower, but it's also Mount Meru, ringed by the Sea of Creation.

The central tower's only entrance, at least for human beings, is a door located at the top of laterite steps that now face the priest. They are very steep, hard to climb, as the way to heaven always is. Sadashiva ascends. At the top, inside, standing upright in a wood-ceilinged chamber that is just big enough for a few people to enter at once, is the *linga*. In this stone shaft lie Shiva's ability to destroy, to chart events, to build, all powers which can serve earthly leaders as well.

The priest kneels and begins a prayer. But then he stops. He feels his mind is clouded. It is not in a fit state of calm and humility to be in the presence of the lord Shiva.

The priest turns around and descends the steps.

A novice from the north ashram, who has been tending a shrine in one of the galleries, takes note: usually the master spends much longer inside.

Apsaras at Angkor Wat.

Chapter III – An Empire Built and Lost

There is no record of when Sadashiva died. But however long his life extended, it fell roughly at the midpoint of Angkorian glory. The empire he knew already ruled much of the Southeast Asian mainland. It had conquering armies, elephant processions, court dancers, carved teak palaces. And, of course, great temples, including the most spectacularly situated of all the Khmers' creations, Preah Vihear, the holy sanctuary atop a 525-metre cliff.[1] How was it possible to build such things? Today, most everyone who visits Cambodia wonders that. The answer seems to be a near-perfect combination of fertile fields, creative minds, strong backs and devotion to heaven.

These qualities all came together on rice-growing estates such as Sadashiva's, the political building blocks of the empire. The estate's lands and people were tasked to support not a castle, but a temple and the gods who inhabited it. Everyone, whether farmers tending rice seedlings in some of the world's best soil, villagers plucking weeds from paving stone cracks or abbots chanting prayers in inner sanctuaries, had a calling as servant of the divine. Each person worked to make the present life better for everyone but was also driven by a personal incentive, because whatever the labour, it would give the person the protection of spirits and perhaps accrue merit for a higher rebirth in the next life.

There was a similar symbiosis at the national level. Estates sent food and implements to the capital to sustain kings and priests and concubines and a host of functionaries, servants and guards. In return came protection, rights to land, blessings from the empire's most powerful priests, and on special occasions, gifts. When Sdok Kok Thom was consecrated in 1052, contributions arriving from the capital included black-eared stallions, a gold palanquin with a three-headed carved serpent, gems, drinking cups, pitchers, garments for monks and a huge supply of dried ginger.

Construction of the capital's great 'mountain temples,' representations of Mount Meru, home of the gods, brought the most dramatic showcasing of this cooperation. I think we can put aside theories that the muscle was provided largely by slaves. To me, the only way by which people could have given so thoroughly of themselves is if the reward was not avoidance of the whip but favour from heaven. Khmers turned out generation after generation

---

[1] Much of the temple as it exists today was added in the 12th century.

to drag, carve and heft into place millions of sandstone and laterite blocks. Aided only by hand tools and elephants, they dug canals and reservoirs that would seem a tall order even with bulldozers and backhoes. The empire did have its coups and rebellions, but the fact that so many enormous projects were carried through to completion suggests that society was by and large stable, peaceful, held together by common values and yearning for a higher life at rebirth.

So Sadashiva's times were rife with glory but they are little known today compared to the second half of the empire's history. That is mostly because the grandest of the temples, the ones most heavily visited today, went up in the later period, as kings continued a game of architectural one-upsmanship of building bigger and higher than the predecessors. In addition, the empire's second half was better supplied with big personalities and historical drama, at least that we know about today. And for the first time we can see real-life Khmers, captured in stone on bas reliefs, a medium that in past ages had displayed only deities.

The last king whom the priest served, Udayadityavarman II, built a great three-tiered pyramid temple, the Baphuon, and died around 1066. There followed a period of short, less memorable reigns until 1113, when one of the most dynamic of all Khmer rulers, Suryavarman II, seized power in a series of coups. In an inscription, he was likened to the bird god Garuda, bounding onto the back of an elephant carrying an enemy king and killing him on the spot. In his approximately thirty-five years on the throne, he tied the empire more tightly together. He fought wars in the west against the Siamese and in the east against the Chams, members of a fellow Hindu culture, and the Annamites, ancestors of today's Vietnamese.

He is best known, however, as builder of Angkor Wat, which to this day is the largest religious structure in the world. It rises in three tiers to a five-peaked summit, its shape and proportions so perfect that spiritual reverie breaks out in all but the most committed sceptics. In its roughly eight hundred metres of bas reliefs, we see the king himself. In one scene, he sits atop his royal dais, surrounded by priests and ministers. Parasols, symbols of rank, flutter overhead. Elsewhere, he strikes a pose atop a war elephant that walks in procession with spearmen and horse-mounted officers. It is the first time the Khmers chose to preserve images of a king and his court and soldiers.

Suryavarman II's death around 1150 brought on a period of palace intrigue and national weakening. In 1177, the Chams took

An Empire Built and Lost

King Suryavarman II, Angkor Wat bas relief.

advantage with a daring attack on the capital. Their war boats stole across the Tonle Sap, the huge lake that lies at the heart of the homeland. The Khmers were caught unprepared. The capital fell and Chams ruled as occupiers for the next four years. Then another great Khmer king appeared, Jayavarman VII. Rallying Khmer forces, he defeated the Chams with a series of land and naval attacks and pursued them back to their own lands. The empire was restored. But the king was just getting started. With the borders secure, he set in motion the biggest building program in all Khmer history.

The walled, moated city of Angkor Thom, measuring more than three kilometres square; the Bayon temple with its dozens of huge carved faces, smiling smiles of eternal serenity; the walled holy complexes of Preah Khan and Ta Prom – all are fruits of Jayavarman VII's reign. So are many lesser known temples and more than a hundred structures in the hinterland that appear to have been hospitals or traveller way stations. Grand scale was matched by devotion to detail. Countless artisans carved worshippers, deities, floral patterns. Bas relief sculptors got even more freedom, beginning a sort of Khmer realism movement. Depicted on the Bayon's walls are a naval battle, with sailors pulling on the oars of war boats, the dead sinking in the water, and archers loosing arrows. Back on land, a couple of thieves steal fruit from a dozing vender, a woman gives birth, fighting cocks go at each other before cheering men.

Then – stagnation. After Jayavarman VII died around 1220, the Khmers built hardly anything. They largely stopped chiselling inscriptions. Society turned to living off its capital. Zhou Daguan, the Chinese envoy who arrived in 1296, witnessed royal pageantry and fireworks and mass bathing in the rivers (he was astounded that the women showed no shame in throwing off their garments to enter the water). Most of the people he describes hardly seem capable of being fierce warriors. Likely the borders were already contracting, as the expanding kingdom of Siam to the west applied new pressure. In 1431 a Siamese army overran Angkor. This time there was no heroic turn around. At some point the Khmer royal family decamped to the region of today's Cambodian capital, Phnom Penh, where they presided over a vastly shrunken state. The great monuments of Angkor were left to gods and jungle.

It's hard to express how much academic brainpower has been applied to explaining how people could have walked away from such things. Military pressure from the Siamese is of course a possible factor. A shift from Hinduism to a more otherworldly Buddhism has been cited, as has evidence of a long-term drought crippling fields. Desire to relocate to the Mekong River for easier foreign trade is another possibility. But many scholars believe that the root cause was in Khmer society itself. The empire had hollowed itself out. Over the course of six centuries, its people had built too much. Toward the end, they found it impossible to keep up the temples and reservoirs, the highways and bridges. They could no longer support the thousands upon thousands of nobles, retainers, soldiers and seers in the capital. In this view, the Siamese military successes were only the final factor in causing collapse and a migration eastward.

In the 1950s, the French scholar Bernard-Philippe Groslier proposed that the decline's root cause was the silting-up of canals and reservoirs that he saw as forming an irrigation network that enabled multiple annual rice crops. More recently, the Greater Angkor Project, an international research consortium, applied airborne radar technology to the question and reached similar conclusions, that what did in the Khmers was their own diligence. In addition to building all those temples, they altered the very face of nature. They created the largest low-density population centre of the pre-industrial world, the Greater Angkor Project concluded, a vast swath of close-together villages extending far beyond the temple zone. They dug reservoirs and canals, built long embankments to direct the flow of water and carry roads. They elevated entire areas as sites where villages could stand safe from seasonal flood waters. They felled huge tracts of forest and sapped the topsoil. Erosion set in. Here and there, researchers found evidence of water breaching dikes late in the empire's history, of ad hoc repairs to those dikes, suggesting that the hydraulic system became increasingly unmanageable as it aged.

After the 15th century, tropical foliage, bats and rain water became the new masters of Angkor. They were rarely respectful of their charge. Tree roots split the carefully fitted stones. To bats, the galleries and worship chambers seemed like caves, so they nested there by the millions, depositing huge quantities of dung that ate away at the sandstone. And year after year, raindrops kept up the attack from above. Some of the towers, celebrations of carved detail when first built, came to resemble melted wax.

Ruination was hastened by one of the Khmers' few shortcomings as builders, inattention to foundations. Beneath the central cores of mountain temples lay nothing more than piles of dirt and rubble. Below massive perimeter walls were mere blocks of laterite or beds of sand, unable to bear the enormous loads entrusted to them. During the empire's final surge of construction under Jayavarman VII, foundations got even shorter shrift. Modern politicians neglect road maintenance knowing potholes won't show up until they're out of office. In a similar way, Jayavarman's engineers cut back on foundations, perhaps to meet otherwise impossible construction deadlines. The king, inspecting the finished edifice, would have never known there was a problem.

One by one, towers came down in thunderous collapses. Roots and lichen went to work on newly exposed stone; the bats moved on to the next tower.

Sketch by Louis Delaporte depicting Angkor in the 1870s.

Chapter IV – The Naturalist

Angkor was no longer the capital, but in Cambodia it was never forgotten. For one thing, though Angkor lost its kings it never lost all its farmers. In the scattered villages that remained in the area, new generations of Khmers grew up knowing that if they wandered into the forest they would come across giant stone faces. In any case, the largest of the temples, Angkor Wat, appears never to have been abandoned. Converted into a Buddhist monastery, it was tended by monks who did a valiant job of keeping the vegetation at bay in that one very large place.

In about the year 1550, one of the kings of the drastically slimmed-down Khmer state is said to have set out on a hunting expedition from his capital far to the east. He came across the shrouded Angkor Thom city and gave orders to clear the vegetation. Five to six thousand men went to work, according to an account written later in the century. 'After everything had been carefully cleaned, the king entered the interior, and having gone all over it, was struck in admiration by the extent of these constructions. And for this reason, he immediately decided to bring his court here, because, in addition to the town being most majestic in its layout, it was sited in one of the finest places on earth, with coppices, rivers and excellent water sources.' There is archaeological confirmation of such a restoration, bas reliefs that were added to Angkor Wat in this period. It is unclear how long the Khmer court stayed. Certainly by around 1750 it had left again, turning most of the monuments back over to the foliage.

Nor was Angkor entirely forgotten by the outside world during this period. Every so often, someone from as far away as Europe made a visit. The story of the hunting king, in fact, is apparently the second-hand report of a Franciscan cleric who was in Angkor around 1585. The rise of colonialism in the 19th century brought increasing numbers of Westerners to the region. Europeans who took up residence in Cambodia gradually became aware of stories of something amazing deep in the interior. A few went to see for themselves. But the world didn't really wake up to the place until Henri Mouhot made the trip.

He was a Frenchman by birth, a traveller by temperament. Born in 1826, he went at age eighteen to Russia, where he tutored nobles in the French language and taught at a military academy. He became interested in botany. He married an English woman who was a descendant of Mungo Park, a Scottish doctor who had died while trying to chart the course of the Niger River. Taking up residence in London, the couple became part of intellectual circles in which the tropics and exploration were all the talk. They got involved with the Royal Geographical Society. In April 1858, with encouragement from society members, though apparently not financial support, Mouhot said goodbye to his wife and set sail for Southeast Asia to try his hand at an expedition himself. He would scout for new forms of flora and fauna.

He established himself in Bangkok, and from there made four extended journeys around Siam, Cambodia and Laos, collecting specimens and keeping a detailed diary of people, places and things he encountered. An etching of the time, based on one of his own sketches from the trail, shows him as the consummate Victorian explorer. Wearing a broad-brimmed hat, he sits alone beneath a tree, making notes or sketches on a board in his lap. A rifle is at his side. Behind him, pack elephants are settling in for the night, while local guides are caught in the glow of a campfire, preparing the evening meal.

In the spring of 1859, Mouhot recounted in the diary, he and his travelling party entered Cambodia at the riverside town of Kampot just a short distance inland from the Gulf of Siam. The king, Ang Duang, was in his royal barge on the river at the time, reclining on a thick cushion with a dozen young girls around him, and saw the foreigner on the shore. The king ordered the boat to come near to ask who this man was. Thus the king received Mouhot, who presented him with an English curiosity of the time, a walking stick that was also a gun. The king granted permission for passage to the former royal capital of Udong. There Mouhot met the country's crown prince, Norodom, who provided elephants and carts for continuation of the journey.

Such was the entrée accorded a young foreigner who had no great rank or reputation back home. Part of the reason was likely curiosity, but perhaps a bigger consideration was that several years earlier King Ang Duang had written France inquiring if it might provide help against Siam and Vietnam, which by then had gobbled up whole swathes of the Cambodian nation, burned the capital more than once, and reduced the royal court to near helplessness. France was now in control down the Mekong, having established colonial rule in parts of southern Vietnam. It had yet to offer 'help' to Cambodia, but here was a Frenchman coming to call. King and farmers alike were watching closely for clues to what his powerful country might do next.

Mouhot and his party continued their travels and in the second half of 1861 arrived in the Laotian royal city of Luang Prabang on the upper reaches of the Mekong River. He pressed further north, ever game to see what lay beyond the next ridge. Mouhot took part in a rhino hunt. A villager bravely lanced the beast; Mouhot was invited to deliver the coup de grace, which he did by piercing its throat with a bayonet (in his diary he recounted this somewhat apologetically, saying that he didn't much like hunting). This was to be about as far north as he got. Laotian authorities, likely suspicious of the man's intentions, sent word that he must go no further. He obeyed. But on the return trek toward Luang Prabang, he fell ill with fever. With the city still some distance away, he made camp on the banks of the Khan River. On 10 November 1861, he died in that camp. He was buried there; a small tomb today marks the site.

His name entered history because a Chinese servant gathered up his personal things, diary included, and brought them out of the forest. The diary eventually made its way back to London. There Mouhot's widow was petitioning the geographical society for a pension, declaring that she was destitute because all the couple's resources had gone to underwrite the expedition. The society demurred, but by some accounts its officials went out of their way to see to publication of the diary in hopes of putting some money into Mrs. Mouhot's purse. First to bring it out, in serial form, was the French journal *Tour du Monde*, in 1863. English and French language book versions followed.

Together they created a sensation. Not because of the nature studies that had been the journeys' purpose but because of Angkor. It turned out that Mouhot had spent three weeks among the ruins early in 1860, drawing maps and sketches, noting down his impressions. The diary revealed him as a perceptive observer and evocative writer, comfortable with metaphor and flights of romantic rhetoric that at times feel like a monologue from a Victorian stage.

Here is Mouhot on Angkor Wat:

> *One of these temples – a rival to that of Solomon and erected by some ancient Michael Angelo – might take an honourable place beside our most beautiful buildings. It is grander than anything left to us by Greece or Rome.*

The temple, he writes, is

> *the first which presents itself to the eye of the traveller, making him forget all the fatigues of the journey, filling him with admiration and delight, such as would be experienced on finding a verdant oasis in the sandy desert. Suddenly, and as if by enchantment, he seems to be transported from barbarism to civilization, from profound darkness to light.*

> *...All the mouldings, sculptures, and bas-reliefs appear to have been executed after the erection of the building. The stones are everywhere fitted together in so perfect a manner that you can scarcely see where are the joinings; there is neither sign of mortar nor mark of the chisel, the surface being as polished as marble. Was this incomparable edifice the work of a single genius, who conceived the idea, and watched over the execution of it? One is tempted to think so; for no part of it is deficient, faulty, or inconsistent.*

All through the Angkor entries are expressions of frustration that he could not know who built and used these fabulous monuments, or how, or when. Gazing down on Angkor Wat from a nearby hilltop, he issues a lamentation, as if sensing that he is surrounded by ghosts.

> *Sad fragility of human things! How many centuries and thousands of generations have passed away, of which history, probably, will never tell us anything: what riches and treasures of art will remain for ever buried beneath these ruins; how many distinguished men – artists, sovereigns and warriors – whose names were worthy of immortality, are now forgotten, laid to rest under the thick dust which covers these tombs!*

Such declarations notwithstanding, Mouhot as a man of scientific outlook did make some effort to uncover the past. He questioned local Cambodians. 'There exists a tradition of a leprous king,' he wrote, 'to whom is attributed the commencement of the great temple, but all else is totally forgotten.' But most every other answer that local people provided concerning the origins of Angkor Wat seems to have left him wincing: "'It is the work of Pra-Eun, the king of the angels;" "It is the work of the giants;"..."It made itself.'"

With no facts in hand, Mouhot let himself engage in some speculation. Angkor must have been built by a people who entered the region from somewhere else, perhaps China, and had now died out, he reasoned. To him it seemed out of the question that the forbears of Cambodians he encountered in the 'barbarous' villages around Angkor could have built it.

With observations like those, Mouhot established a conflict of outlook that endures down to the present day. The French treated Angkor as an archaeological site, the vestige of an advanced ancient people, its past legitimately open to empirical investigation and analysis. Cambodians were more likely to see Angkor as a supernatural realm whose origins and great events humans could never know, and indeed might have no right to.

With the diary's publication, intellectuals in Europe and the United States had a fabulous new lost civilisation about which to rave and speculate. Some of them went to see for themselves. The first photographs circulated in Europe. Etchings of the giant faces of Angkor became popular fare in newspapers and magazines. Sculpture, carried off by some of these early visitors, went on display in expos and museums back home, as did some early and unreadable inscription rubbings. Meanwhile, local Cambodians working under French taskmasters began the first efforts at clearing some of the jungle away, no doubt first kneeling and addressing prayers to local spirits: please forgive us for disturbing your habitation. We mean no harm. We want only to earn money to feed our families.

In Western salons and lecture halls there was continuing frustration that still virtually nothing was known of the civilisation's provenance, its history or the personalities who shaped it. Eurocentric theories were tossed around right and left: Angkor is the work of one of the Twelve Tribes of Israel. No, it was built by Alexander the Great.

In the end, what started to clear the fog were things that Mouhot mentioned only very briefly: inscriptions. In some ruins, he observed, chiselled writing covered entire columns. He could not read a word, however. The inscriptions are 'as a sealed book for want of an interpreter,' he wrote, 'and they may, perchance throw light on the subject when some European savant shall succeed in deciphering them.'

Étienne Aymonier as a young military man. Courtesy of Bernard Kessler.

Chapter V – The Linguist

It took years, but Mouhot's hoped-for savant finally reached the scene. His name was Étienne-François Aymonier.

He stepped off a ship in Saigon, Vietnam, in October 1869, age twenty-five, a newly commissioned sub-lieutenant in the French marines. A native of the alpine Savoie region, he had entered military service as a teenager, standing in for a brother who had drawn a 'bad number' in the conscription system.[1] Desire for an advanced education appears to have partly motivated this substitution – from the start of his military career, Aymonier showed more enthusiasm for books than soldiering. Shortly after being promoted to corporal, he was assigned to his regiment's library, where away from the bustle of martial life he studied Latin and made his way through the works of Rousseau, Dumas and other French writers. He studied algebra and geometry, winning academic honours. 'Corporal, you carried off the prizes on a bayonet,' an acquaintance told him. Later he gained admission to the famed military academy St. Cyr and after more study was commissioned an officer. Finally his long education came to an end, and he headed east with members of his regiment. A ship delivered the men to Egypt, where they travelled by rail to the Red Sea (the Suez Canal was in its final months of construction). A second ship took the soldiers across the Indian Ocean toward Indochina.

Huge expanses of Southeast Asia were now in European hands. Only Siam would remain independent. France was now master of Cambodia as well as southern Vietnam and on its way to ruling the north. Laos was in its sights. Britain had Singapore, Brunei and parts of Burma and the Malayan peninsula, Spain had the Philippines and the Netherlands had parts of what is now Indonesia. The new authorities were applying the mix of modernisation and exploitation that became the hallmark of European colonialism. They organised the local economies to benefit the ones back home. They began creating such institutions as ports, schools and courts.

---

[1] This and many other details of Aymonier's life and work in this chapter and the next are taken from private materials kindly provided by Bernard Kessler, a great nephew of Aymonier. These materials included letters that Aymonier wrote to his family during his time in Indochina, an unpublished memoir, photographs and family recollections shared by Mr. Kessler, who as a boy went many times to the Paris apartment in which his illustrious great uncle had lived. I have also drawn on Aymonier's extensive published writings and on accounts by other authors.

The process was overseen by a corps of colonial administrators, many of them green young men in their twenties, just out of school back in Europe.

Judging by his own accounts, Aymonier was something of a duck out of water in his first weeks in Saigon, disapproving and disbelieving of much of what he saw, a bit homesick, likely yearning in the tropical heat for the bracing airs of his native village, Chatelard. In his first letter to his brother Felix, he expressed disappointment that no letter was awaiting him on arrival: 'A sheet of paper, an envelope, a stamp, half an hour, are after all not sacrifices so large.' The gravel streets of Saigon were too narrow, in Sub-Lieutenant Aymonier's view, though they did have some nice purple-flowered trees. Vietnamese he met had 'hideous mouths,' teeth stained in black, lips encrusted in betel. One day he awoke to find that a snake had slithered into his ground-floor bedroom through a window. He dispatched it with a sabre.

Perhaps he was experiencing what today we would call culture shock. But as he settled into his new life, there took hold in him a deep curiosity about the society in which he was now living, an openness and respect found in few colonial officials. He soon transferred out of military duty to civilian administration. Assigned to Vietnam's Mekong Delta province of Travinh, home of a large ethnic Cambodian population, he got his first exposure to a culture and heritage that would entrance him. While working his way through such positions as Inspector, Fourth Class and Auxiliary Administrator, Second Class, he studied and mastered the Cambodian language, an accomplishment all the more difficult in view of lack of books and courses of instruction. By 1874, he was teaching Cambodian to other French officers and publishing a French-Cambodian dictionary. He would also learn the equally unstudied language of the Chams, the people who had captured Angkor in 1177 but in subsequent centuries lost their state and slipped into largely powerless minority status in Vietnam and Cambodia.

Like any number of Frenchmen serving in the colonies, Aymonier lived with a local woman during his stay in Indochina. The woman was a Cham princess, and she gave birth to a son. That boy grew up to be a senior officer in the Viet Minh army that in 1954 defeated the French at Dien Bien Phu and overturned the colonial order that his father had helped construct.

In Cambodia, that order had formally come into being in 1863. A delegation of French officers sailed up the Mekong in a gunboat and signed an agreement with Norodom, the crown prince who had provisioned Henri Mouhot four years earlier. King Ang Duang was now dead and Norodom the ranking royal, but he had not been crowned due to obstruction from Siam. The French offered protection to the king and kingdom but of course there was plenty in the deal for them as well – rights to trade, to station soldiers, and, in their way of thinking, to civilise a backward society.

The following year, Norodom was crowned. In Cambodia today, he is regarded as the first king of the modern era and something of a tragic hero. Many historians say that his decision to accept the protectorate status, however humiliating, ultimately saved the Cambodian nation from extinction at the hands of its neighbours. And he never gave the French a moment's rest, challenging them at every turn from day one.

Inscription from a temple in Koh Ker.

Norodom resumed his life of royal splendour, moving to a white-walled palace compound by the river in Phnom Penh. There he was tended by ministers, fan bearers, concubines and dancers. Outside the walls there lived a French 'representative' whose humble title belied his powers – he vetted major decisions coming from the court and had recommendations of his own. On 1 January 1879, a new representative was named. It was Étienne Aymonier, now in his middle thirties. He would later write that he took this assignment without enthusiasm, because it required dealing with Norodom. Indeed, when the new representative went to the palace on January 4 to present his credentials, he was handed a letter declaring that the king 'strongly protests' an alleged French failure to provide the original or a certified copy of a certain contract and that due to this issue His Majesty might cut off all communications.

Like most French administrators, Aymonier regarded the king as corrupt and cruel, a wily manipulator who had to be carefully watched and was an enormous economic burden on the Cambodian people. '"The kingdom is made for the king, *who eats it*," says the local expression,' Aymonier wrote in a memoir. The new representative was particularly incensed by Norodom's practice of condemning to death concubines accused of the crime of lèse majesté – a previous French representative had witnessed the execution of seven such women, describing them as a 'seed of Eve's apple.' In his memoir, Aymonier recounts considering taking a squad of armed men to rescue a new batch of the condemned. That did not happen, however. King Norodom backed off from this practice and issued clemency to the women.

But all in all, such tumult appears to have been rare for the new representative. In an 1879 letter home, he recounted a routine, repetitive, even boring existence in what was then a tiny riverside capital. He rose at six, went for a horseback ride or walk on the streets, took a bath, had breakfast, went to the office, knocked off for siesta, and so on. He was in bed by nine. Every Wednesday, an official boat arrived from Saigon. He was not overburdened by work, clearly. It was an ideal situation for devoting extended time to what he really cared about, Khmer culture and antiquity. However contemptuous he was of the country's present-day monarch, he was becoming entranced with the kings and the kingdom of the vanished era. Taking trips outside the capital and up the Mekong, he encountered remarkable stone ruins covered in brush, and clearly felt the same sense of wonder that filled most every European. Given his aptitude in languages, his attention went in particular to the inscriptions that were to be found here and there, carved into ancient stone. Many were perfectly legible after so many centuries, if only one knew how to read their circular letters. Whereas Mouhot threw up his hands, Aymonier rolled up his sleeves. He began making rubbings of the texts and taking them home for study.

Étienne Aymonier (front seat, right). Courtesy of Bernard Kessler.

Most of the Khmer Empire's writings – we can surmise that they included religious epics, liturgical guides, rice production reports and tax rolls – had been kept on palm leaves, which fell victim to the mould and rot of the humid tropical weather. Not one of these had survived through to modern times. But the stone records were durable and, in view of the difficulties of making them, surprisingly common. What Aymonier collected in these early trips outside of Phnom Penh were among the first of more than a thousand Angkorian inscriptions that would eventually be catalogued. They were the primary historical record that the ancient Khmers left behind – 'the Khmer corpus,' as the experts call it.

Cambodians living near the ruins of course knew that the inscriptions existed. But ability to read them had long-ago died out. Many villagers seem to have regarded them, like the stone monuments themselves, as works of the gods, beyond the comprehending powers of human beings. A few learned Buddhist monks in Phnom Penh had been trying to translate some of them by applying their knowledge of another Indian-based language, Pali, the sacred tongue of Buddhism. But these efforts came to little.

Back in Phnom Penh after his excursions, Aymonier could study the rubbings at his leisure. Some of the texts were not that old and he puzzled them out based on his knowledge of the modern Cambodian language. But the older ones were often stumpers.

It had become clear fairly quickly that though there was some variation in the stones' writing systems, all were derived from Indian script used for Sanskrit, the sacred language of Hinduism. Some of the writing, in fact, was especially close to what colonial Dutch scholars had found on Java and nearby islands that had been the home soil for other lost empires of Indian roots, Srivijaya and Majapahit. But when the linguistic lessons of Sanskrit were applied to the stones of Cambodia, some passages just didn't make sense. No number of retranslations straightened things out. Something fundamental about how the ancient Khmers expressed themselves remained a secret.

From this impasse came one of Aymonier's first big contributions to epigraphy, as the study of inscriptions is known.

He later described the break-through as originating in something very small, his efforts to plumb the origins of a single word of modern Cambodian (such was the level of specialisation at which he routinely operated). The word was *gamaten*, often translated as 'high lord.' Cambodian men of letters classified it as derived from Sanskrit but Aymonier wasn't so sure. To him it didn't seem to fit the linguistic patterns of other three-syllable Sanskrit-origin words.

The epiphany happened as he pored over a rubbing that another Frenchman had made years earlier at the great Bayon temple, centrepiece of the walled city Angkor Thom. 'It was not without real emotion,' he later recounted, 'when all of a sudden, one day in March 1879, I read in a spindly, mediocre copy of a Bayon inscription... this expression: *Kamraten jagat*. The first word was in a context that implied 'high lord.' *Kamraten*, Aymonier grasped that day, was *gamaten* in ancient form. The two words had similar meaning and sound despite the centuries of linguistic evolution separating them.

From this first connection came a realisation that would make possible the full reading of the records of the empire's past: Sanskrit-like letters on Khmer inscription stones did not always spell out Sanskrit words. The ancient Khmers had adapted Sanskrit letters to record their own common language of the time. On that day in 1879, Aymonier had recognised and translated the first word of that tongue. It is known today as Old Khmer, predecessor of modern Cambodian. Aymonier later designated *gamraten* as its very first word to be decoded.

Aymonier never became fully proficient in Sanskrit but he pressed ahead with Old Khmer and for many years was the world's leading expert in it, indeed, possibly the only one. In an article published in 1881, he drew on various Old Khmer inscriptions to take a first crack at one of the most basic of questions facing historians: what was the sequence of Angkor's kings and when did they rule? Writing for a colonial journal in Saigon that normally focused on such subjects as harbour development and legal codes, he proposed that the ancient empire's 'time of splendour' ran from the 8th century to the 11th century and was dominated by three great kings, all of a single dynasty. He named them as Yaço Varman, Jaya Varman and Surya Varman and proposed dates for their times on the throne.

We know today that there were in fact kings bearing those names. We know also that they ruled in that order, though '*varman*' did not indicate that were part of a single dynasty – it was instead a suffix that meant 'shield' or 'protector' and was a standard part of kings' names. Nor did Aymonier get all the dates correct and he did not have the names of the many other kings who reigned in between the three. But how can he be faulted? He was providing the first glimmerings into the personalities and dates of the fabled past.

In May 1881, Aymonier arrived back in France for an extended visit. He encountered quite some enthusiasm for his favourite subject, epigraphy, and not only among the corps of Sanskrit scholars that was taking form in the universities of France and other

European colonial powers. Newspapers and academic journals had kept up with reports of the finding of mysterious stone writings. Rubbings had gone on display as exotic artefacts at some of the industrial and cultural expositions that were in fashion in late 19th century Europe. Now Aymonier added to the supply, handing over to scholars fifty-four rubbings that he had made. They quickly became the object of intense study, but everyone wished there were more, and that the reproduction method was better to allow a more accurate reading.

While visiting his home region of Savoie, Aymonier met with an official who told him that the Ministry of Public Instruction wanted to send someone on a formal scientific mission to collect as many high-quality inscription reproductions as possible. If he wanted the job, it was his. He said yes.

Before leaving France, Aymonier underwent training in how to create high-quality inscription copies using a technique pioneered by the French archaeologist Victor Lottin de Laval. It was well suited to rural Southeast Asia, requiring only water and easily obtainable materials such as paper and sponges. The stone is first cleaned. Then wet paper is rubbed onto its surface with a sponge, sinking into the grooves of individual letters. When the paper is removed, the ancient message stands out. The resulting *estampage* is generally easier to read than a photograph. Indeed, even in the age of the digital camera, variations on this medium remain in use among inscription specialists.

So in February 1882, Aymonier again stepped off a ship in Saigon. After consultations with French authorities, he proceeded to Phnom Penh – he was no longer French representative there, rather a government-commissioned researcher whom everyone was supposed to help. On March 20, he set out from the city, transport courtesy of two elephants provided by his old nemesis King Norodom.[2] Accompanying were four Cambodians, a Chinese

---

[2] While Aymonier was off on his inscription mission, one of the greatest palace dramas and challenges to French authority broke out. In 1884, the French governor general in Saigon, exasperated over what he viewed as Norodom's obstructionism and petulance, arrived by gunboat with a force of French and Vietnamese soldiers, personally turned Norodom out of bed (the Frenchman kicked an attendant who tried the block the way, the attendant later wrote) and forced him to sign papers drastically expanding the 1863 protectorate agreement. Within months, widespread rebellion broke out in the countryside. After more than a year of military operations the French proved unable to quell it and were forced to approach Norodom hat in hand for help. In return for the French backing off from earlier demands for full control, Norodom persuaded the rebels to give up the fight.

servant and a fellow French officer who kept with the group only part of the way. For the next three and a half years, the team crisscrossed Cambodia, former Khmer areas of Siam and former Cham parts of Vietnam to visit hundreds of sites associated with antiquity. Sometimes Aymonier left behind elephants to ride in the relative comfort of colonial steamboats (the company operating them gave the team fifty percent discounts on tickets). Other times travel was by pirogue, through waters so shallow from dry season drought that rowers stuck their paddles into the bottom like poles. On land it could be again by elephant or by oxcart or foot. As colonial master, Aymonier had it easier than the Cambodians and his servant, no doubt, but that doesn't say much. There was at all times the threat of snakes – he killed at least one personally – and tigers. There was the danger of malaria and cholera, not to mention dysentery, a disease which had earlier hospitalised him. On the trail he ate no bread for long stretches, only rice. He went weeks without speaking French. He would recount later that he began thinking in Cambodian. Through such exploits he became something of a exploration celebrity back in France, with his latest letters and locations reported admiringly in publications of the Société de géographie.

At some of his stops, Aymonier collected ancient sculpture. In the main hall of the Musée Guimet in Paris today, you can see some of those pieces. Most are heads and free-standing statues, suggesting a straight-forward taste in art. But there is also a large and detailed 'Churning of the Sea of Milk,' the classic scene from Hindu mythology in which gods and demons work together to create the Elixir of Immortality. This would have taken up quite a bit of space in an oxcart.

The museum marks many of his pieces as *'provenance inconnu,'* provenance unknown. Does this mean that Aymonier bought them from people he met in the districts he visited, and afterwards showed a scholar's caution in reporting that he couldn't say for sure where they had come from? I like to think so. It feels better than picturing him personally sawing off the heads of eight century-old statues, something that the colonial mindset rationalised as an act of protection, a way to further archaeology and preserve history.[3]

---

[3] Other times, it was theft plain and simple and this was sometimes prosecuted. In 1923, the French writer and adventurer André Malraux clumsily hacked bas reliefs from Banteay Srey temple with the idea of selling them to American collectors. He was arrested and convicted, but managed to escape serving a sentence. He later incorporated this episode into a novel, known in English as *The Royal Way*.

Still, inscriptions and supplies for the wet and messy process of making copies were always the focus on the Aymonier travels.

I can picture a particular encounter happening over and over: Aymonier arrives with his team at a village and asks to speak with the headman. We hear there's a ruin nearby, he says, sipping tea that has been placed before him as an important visitor. Does it have ancient writing? Yes? Can you show us exactly where? And off they go to the stone. More sheets of paper are wet down, rubbed onto the stone and soon there are three or four portable records of another message that hasn't been read in centuries. The next morning, as the team prepares to leave, the stampings have been rolled up and their origin carefully annotated. Several more pages have been filled in one of the large notebooks in which Aymonier kept his *journal de marche*. The team moves out of the village, and soon its people get to talking: Let us hope that the Frenchman did not anger the temple's resident spirit. And can he really read the words of Heaven?

Étienne Aymonier later in life. Courtesy of Bernard Kessler.

The inner courtyard's western *gopura*, in this photo from around 1970. Aymonier would have seen the *gopura* in this largely intact condition when he visited in 1883. Courtesy of Muang Boran Data Center.

Chapter VI – Mission to Sdok Kok Thom

October 1882 found Aymonier in Saigon, overseeing shipment to France of the physical gleanings of a survey he'd just completed in north and central Cambodia – statues, pottery, prints and a few actual inscription stones. 'My health is good,' he wrote his brother Felix. Next, he said, 'I am going to make a long visit in the region of Angkor and Battambang.' On November 17 he left Saigon, travelled by steamboat up the Mekong, then into Cambodia's Great Lake, the Tonle Sap. He disembarked near Angkor, along with a group of Europeans who'd come for a look at the monuments. Even in 1882 the place was drawing Western tourists. As December ran its course, Aymonier went out in the relatively cool air of the season to examine a number of lesser-known ruins of Angkor. Then he left for areas northwest of the Great Lake, including Sisophon province.

Sadashiva's temple lay in Sisophon.

There are no records of anything that happened at Sdok Kok Thom in the eight hundred years that had passed since the time of the Brahmin priest. After his death, probably the temple continued for many years as the district's focus of Hindu worship. As Buddhism spread in the 12th century, perhaps it was converted for the rites of that faith. At some point, Khmer political authority gave way to Siamese. At an equally unknown time the great estate that the priest had overseen collapsed. Its people dispersed. The temple was given over to the elements; foliage and animals moved in. But, as at Angkor, those few villagers who remained in the area knew that they had a fantastic neighbour. People began calling the stone place in the forest not by its onetime Sanskrit name but by one in their own language. It became Prasat Sdok Kok Thom, Temple of the Great Reed Lake. That was an apparent reference to the holy reservoir, which, though no longer tended by a corps of caretakers, continued faithfully to collect water and to sustain large expanses of reeds.

In mid-January 1883, Aymonier reached the village of Svay Chek, then headed west along an ancient Angkorian road that was still largely passable by cart though hardly used any more. It had no settlements along it. A traveller in these parts, he wrote later, was more likely to run into wild beasts and brigands than Siamese policemen.

Drawing near the temple, he made his trademark methodical observations about distance and direction to various towns in the district. As for the temple itself he had this to say in a book he wrote years later:

> *One finds it on the eastern edge of a forest which is denser and higher than the forests which prevail for three leagues from east to west.*

He noted the holy reservoir (though overstating its dimensions – he may merely have estimated). He recorded the existence of the processional avenue, the walls, the eastern gates. To me his account of the architecture betrays a touch of boredom. He had, after all, seen the grandest the Khmers had to offer.

He entered the central courtyard, observing that the north library was better preserved than the south. Finally he came to the main sanctuary, where Sadashiva had tended the holy *linga*.

> *Partly ruined, this tower is still about ten metres high...At the edge of this tower lie some fragments of statues of Brahmin gods or goddesses which are nothing particularly remarkable.*

But then, something that *was* remarkable: a stone monolith – a *stele* is the technical word – standing almost as tall as the visitor, its four sides crammed with hundreds of lines of Sanskrit and Old Khmer. It would have been immediately clear that this was one of the longest, most comprehensive texts ever created by the ancient Khmers. I picture Aymonier standing amazed, perhaps pulling out a magnifying glass to examine this stunning find.

He recounted the stone in far greater detail and technicality than anything he had to say about the temple.

> *The stele of Sdok Kak Thom, which we encountered at the northeast corner of the enclosing galleries, erected on its pedestal, and in all likelihood in the same place where it was put up... was carved in a block of grey sandstone of which the grain is of the greatest fineness. ...Its proportions are very elegant. It measures about 1.5 metres high, including trunk, base and pyramidal top....*

> *While not perfect, the state of preservation of the monument is good....Some lines of Sanskrit are a little deteriorated on the top of the first three sides but the text may be almost entirely reconstructed.*

He noted the number of lines on each side, and that the stonecutter had put some trial letters at the base of the stone. He noted how lines of Sanskrit ended with a small symbol, a sort of star. And he saw something curious – as the text moved toward its conclusion, the letters got smaller and smaller. It was is if the stonecutter had not planned the layout well or midway through the job had been given extra material to include.

The script of the Sanskrit passages was beautiful, Aymonier said, but aesthetically not really in a class of its own. As for the writing in the other language:

Nothing is comparable to the extraordinary craftsmanship, to the marvellous steadiness of the tracing of the Khmer section of this stele of Sdok Kak Thom.

During the visit, Aymonier made three, possibly four estampages of all four faces of the stone. Soon he and his team moved on. By February 10 they were in the relative comforts of the western town of Battambang. 'Lots of inscriptions to decipher,' he wrote his brother Felix from Battambang, summing up the previous weeks' accomplishments. 'A beautiful work, a fascinating mission...that has the advantage of distancing me from the world here.'

With breaks in Saigon, the travels and work continued through 1883, 1884 and into 1885. In July that year, Aymonier and his team arrived in Qui Nhon, central Vietnam, to survey temples and inscriptions left by Chams who had ruled the area in Angkorian times. But there the work abruptly ended – Vietnamese nationalists staged an uprising against colonial rule. It was suddenly impossible for a Frenchman to travel freely in rural areas. With great regret, Aymonier ended the mission. He boarded a ship for another trip back to France, no doubt frustrated, but having the satisfaction of knowing he'd reached almost every site he wanted.

And certainly epigraphers back in his home country already had plenty to work with, thanks to his efforts. Sanskrit scholar Louis Finot later wrote that with publication of the 'splendid harvest of epigraphy' that Aymonier had collected, 'the fog of legend that had concealed the past of Indochina cleared away as if by magic to reveal in a single stroke five centuries of history.'

The fog's dissipation may have occurred quickly, but publication did not. Within a year of Aymonier's survey of Sdok Kok Thom, only the inscription's existence and a bit of the content had become known in academic circles in Europe. In an article published in January 1884, the Sanskrit scholar Abel Bergaigne made reference to its great length – 'the wordiness of official poets carries on from era to era' – and observed that Khmer inscription carvers, unable to infinitely expand the size of the stones, had resorted to making the letters on them smaller.

In 1886, Aymonier was back in Indochina, this time serving as colonial resident in Binh Thuan, a province of Vietnam. Here his duties were as far removed from scholarly inquiry as imaginable – he was closely involved in French efforts to suppress the continuing rebellion. After two years, he returned permanently to France, a move he later attributed to bad health. There he became the first head of the newly formed École coloniale. His administrative duties and an initial academic focus on things Cham led his Cambodian work to be pushed back. Year after year he published no full translation of the inscription. In the meantime, he engaged in what may have been a little academic protectionism. I find it intriguing that in a detailed description of his Cambodia peregrinations that he published in 1892, he never mentions Sdok Kok Thom. He notes an extended stop at the nearby Svay Chek and visits to 'several other ruins' in the area. A map with a dotted line of travel shows an excursion to the west, where Sdok Kok Thom is located, but no notation of its presence there. Divers seeking sunken treasure never reveal the location of a find until they're done with it. I wonder if Aymonier wanted to keep the temple's location quiet for the time being, lest someone else go there and beat him to the punch with a translation, at least of the Sanskrit passages. Some of his letters allude to tensions with other scholars (one letter mentions one as being 'furious' with the success of his inscription-collecting mission). The dons of French academia, holders of multiple advanced degrees in Asian languages, literature and history, seem at times to have taken a patronising tone toward a man who on subjects Asian was largely self-taught.[1]

---

[1] In 1903 and 1904, Aymonier engaged in an extended published exchange of riposte and counter-riposte with a sinologist named Paul Pelliot. The subject was the pre-Angkorian state of Funan. Pelliot questioned many aspects of Aymonier's conclusions about the state, which was known in large part through Chinese annals. According to the epigrapher George Coedès, this very public fight deeply wounded Aymonier's pride for years and led to a rift with the L'École française d'Extrême-Orient, whose official journal had published Pelliot's attacks. In an epitaph written after Aymonier's death in 1929, Coedès settled great praise on the late scholar as a pioneer of Indochinese studies but offered the opinion that his final works were largely a re-arguing of historical points that had long been settled.

Whatever tensions existed with other scholars, Aymonier and the Sanskrit specialist Abel Bergaigne appear to have worked in the closest of harmony. 'M. Aymonier is pursuing with great zeal and perfect understanding the task with which he's been consigned, research of the inscriptions of Cambodia,' Bergaigne wrote in his 1884 journal article that mentioned Sdok Kok Thom. In 1900, Aymonier began the introduction to his three-volume work *Le Cambodge* with a mournful marking of Bergaigne's untimely death twelve years earlier in an Alpine accident, calling it a loss to 'his friends, his country and science.'

But at some point in the 1890s, Aymonier gathered up his notes and began writing what would be the most important work of his career, the three-volume *Le Cambodge*. Volume II, published in 1901, contained the description of his Sdok Kok Thom visit cited above[2] and a detailed translation of the inscription, with commentary. He handled the stone's Old Khmer passages; another scholar, Auguste Barth, did the Sanskrit.

Estampages that Aymonier had made at Sdok Kok Thom eventually found their way to the National Library of France. Rolled up, stored in cardboard boxes, they were examined and re-examined by successive generations of scholars and became the key document for understanding the first half of the Khmer Empire's history.

In October 2009 came a new request for a look, from me. In an electronically locked reading room on the second floor of the library's beaux arts headquarters in central Paris, an archivist brought out an aging cardboard box, Boite 4. Inside, along with other rubbings from the Aymonier expeditions, were four rolls. On a small sheet of paper with the rolls were the words: *Stele de Sdok Kak Thom, à 4 faces, à 4 exemplaires par face. Sanskrit et Khmer*. It was ink, in Aymonier's careful hand.

On a long table, an archivist and I carefully unrolled the cylinders, one at a time. Each contained three copies of one side of the inscription stone, despite Aymonier's notation stating that there were four. All the sheets were in remarkable shape a hundred thirty years later, bearing the clear raised letters of the thousand-year-old chronicle. The diminishing size of the writing, the star-like symbols at the ends of lines, the beauty of the individual letters all were eminently clear, just as described.

Several people who passed through the reading room in the hours I was there sensed that something unusual was on display. They stepped over to ask about it and I had the honour of telling the tale of this remarkable chronicle of this remarkable civilisation.

Had I had it handy, I would have quoted Aymonier's own final assessment of the inscription. In a rare departure from the dry academic prose in which he normally expressed himself, he had this to say in *Le Cambodge*:

> *It is the most extraordinary of all the inscriptions of Cambodia, and even one of the most remarkable memorials that men in any country have ever left behind on stone.*

---

[2] He published a very similar article in the January-February 1901 edition of *Journal Asiatique*. It's unclear which account appeared first.

Doorframe inscription from Preah Ko temple, Hariharalaya.

Chapter VII – Messages from the Past

It's easy to breeze past the Cambodian National Museum's exhibit of inscription stones. Visitors have just seen the largest bronze statue the Khmers ever cast, a spectacular rendering of that familiar scene of Vishnu beneath the Sea of Creation, slumbering (unfortunately minus inlaid moustache and eyebrows). Ahead beckons a hall filled with equally dramatic stone sculpture.

But it's best to hold off and pay some attention to the stones that date to the statues' times and before, as I did on a visit in 2009. Each stone was created, at enormous cost and effort, because someone was determined to leave a specific message, both for the gods, and for us human inhabitants of the future.

One of the oldest stones on display is a rich brown and black, standing about a metre tall. It was commissioned, museum officials believe, by a queen who lived around the year 500 AD. Her name was Kulaprabhavati and she appears to have wanted to memorialise her place in her late husband's heart. 'She was universally known as the beloved of the king, as Saci is for Indra, as Suaha for the Seven-Flamed Fire, as Rudrani for Shiva, as Sri for Vishnu.' In eighteen lines, she reveals herself as an educated woman, citing love pairings of Hindu mythology. In her widowhood, she informs us, she has entrusted herself to Vishnu.

Nearby is a metre and a half-high stone with a crescent moon carved at the top. This one is about piety, but it is also about property. In twenty lines, it reports gifts that were given to Shiva – today we would say to a temple honouring him – by a man named Candrabhanu (whose name begins with the Sanskrit word for moon). He has given eight thousand araca nut trees, coconut palm trees, fruit trees, and slaves to tend them.

Elsewhere is one of the shortest inscriptions the Khmers ever produced: a single Sanskrit word that means 'the lotuses that are Shiva's feet.' Two carved footprints also grace the stone.

Learning Sanskrit and Old Khmer to absorb these things in the original is a lifetime's undertaking. Even if you read in translation, as I do, it can be rough going. The writers can frustrate with lack of directness, with repetitions that have no apparent purpose, with contradictions. Their use of pronouns can leave you guessing as to who's being referred to. And there is of course the assumption that any reader will have the full cultural literacy of the times, recognising, for instance, each of those pairs of perfect lovers cited by that bereaved queen of fifteen hundred years ago.

Many of the Khmers' inscriptions, like these in the museum, were recorded on free-standing stones. Others will never come to a museum, because they are part of the fabric of ancient buildings. The jambs of doors are a favourite place for carved words. Others are found on columns, in window frames, between figures in bas reliefs. Only recently have serious efforts begun to protect these *in situ* texts. For some doorjamb inscriptions, there is a daily threat from tourist shoulders as crowds press through narrow entrances that were intended for priests and kings in single file.

The ancient Khmers were of two minds about the importance of appearance in the stone medium. Some steles were carefully shaped and sanded; others were rough slabs of random proportions, hacked out of a quarry wall. It's the same with the letters themselves. Some are carved with great care, others are a bit haphazard. There are spelling errors. What the Khmers seem to have cared about most were the thoughts and facts being conveyed, not the physical attributes of the words' representation.

Gods of course turn up often in the texts, accompanied by verbal entourages of praise and adoration. In this way, the texts reveal the theology of the times and which beliefs and holy practices passed in and out of observance as history progressed. Royals make frequent appearances too. Sometimes they are the focus of the words, other times they are only mentioned in passing, that king so-and-so was reigning when such-and-such happened. If the stone is dated, the mention of the king gives new understanding of who was in power when. The stone's location is evidence that the ruler's authority extended to that place at that time.

Other texts tell stories. One of my favourites concerns a saintly man who received a royal summons to officiate at a temple. One day, Shiva and a delegation of gods came to visit him. They congratulated the priest on his service and invited him to come to heaven with them. But the man declined this unimaginable honour. He asked instead that Shiva grant a boon, the right for his family to live at the temple for eternity. Shiva agreed. The priest died after selecting his heir.

The typical inscription is relatively short. It might commemorate a particular event, such as creation of a new temple and gifts made to it – land, slaves, dancers, silver bowls, palanquins, fly whisks are commonly mentioned. If the gifts can be expected to generate merit for an elevation in the next life, the texts may specify to whom that merit will go.

Inscriptions on bas reliefs often serve as captions. At Angkor Wat, one identifies by name the worthy who is shown kneeling next to the king, while others, accompanying some horrifying depictions of the thirty-two Hindu hells, detail which class of miscreants will end up in which particular perdition. Those who murder, those who steal from a guru, those who take flowers from Shiva's garden, those who approach other men's wives, those who urinate within temple walls – all have special places awaiting them.

And land is a very common subject. An inscription may state that the fields graciously provided by His Majesty the King extend to a particular canal on the north or holy tree on the west. These texts help illuminate a system in which land was bought or awarded by the king, markers were erected, and ownership energetically defended, with the equivalent of lawsuits being filed against alleged encroachers – some of them were known to move boundary markers. In reading these inscriptions, I often sense the same authority and sense of proprietorship found in papers on file with the clerk in a modern courthouse.

Other stones record the outcome of legal disputes. Thus it is that details have survived about a 10th century case in which a female slave was exchanged for a buffalo, but then ran away. The man who had provided the buffalo wanted compensation. The man who had received the buffalo agreed at first to provide another slave

Hell scene from the bas reliefs at Angkor Wat.
Courtesy of Stephen A. Murphy.

as a replacement, then went back on his word. So the dispute was tried, with the court ruling against the man who'd reneged. In the end, a second slave was given to replace the first.

Curses and threats are often found, levelled against anyone who interferes with the inscription's temple.

In recent years, some archaeologists have focused on the astrological significance in the layout of Khmer temples, seeking to establish whether they were designed as earthly reflections of the movements of planets, moon and sun. Certainly inscriptions show that people of that time paid close attention to the skies. When stating when a particular event happened – the consecration of a *linga*, perhaps – stones may specify not just the date but the time of day, by stating the positions of the planets.

When stones are in two languages, Old Khmer is usually used to convey practical information such as lists of gifts. Praise of gods and ruler is more often a job for Sanskrit, rendered in verse. To understand these passages, readers must synthesise the allusion, double meaning and often convoluted structure that the writers of the time loved. It is the same challenge that comes with deducing the 'real' meaning of an English poem, especially when the poet is no longer around to answer questions.

But once language is sorted out, the job of comprehension is just beginning. Prominent Khmers often had multiple names and titles acquired at different stages of their lives. So is a powerful prince named on one stone perhaps the same man mentioned by another name a decade later? Likewise, a city or mountain may be identified by a name that has now died out. So just where was it?

And then come questions of what to believe. When numbers and dates are involved, the stones are generally quite reliable. For matters such as land ownership and court rulings, every society needs records on which everyone agree. These were those records. When different inscriptions describe the same plot of land, for instance, they rarely contradict each other. Stones take a long time to prepare – there was little opportunity for careless errors to creep in.

But concerning such things as the actions and character of kings, words usually have to be taken as more an expression of ideal than of fact. If a king's sword is described as being red with the blood of enemies, we at least come away knowing that bravery in battle was among the virtues expected in a monarch. If he is recorded as a tireless reader of sacred texts, we know that he at least had to go through the motions.

Scholars also have to consider what's not in an inscription. The archaeologist Charles Higham has written that no Khmer inscription

Messages from the Past

Inscription from a temple in Koh Ker.

makes direct mention of the centralised irrigation system which in Bernard-Philippe Groslier's view formed the basis of state authority. If such a system existed, Higham asks, wouldn't there have been documentation of it somewhere on the stones? But on the other hand, we do have inscriptions that say that reservoirs were created for the 'benefit of society.' Does that mean to provide for society's general spiritual benefit or to bring water to rice fields and keep people in food?

It's a fabulous view of events from a millennium ago, but it's still a view though a keyhole. We have no access to the private thoughts of people from the era. How different from other periods of history: Love letters that Henry VIII wrote to Ann Boleyn, for instance, have survived and can be read today in the Vatican Library.

> *My mistress and friend: I and my heart put ourselves in your hands, begging you to have them [as] suitors for your good favour, and that your affection for them should not grow less through absence. For it would be a great pity to increase their sorrow since absence does it sufficiently, and more than ever I could have thought possible reminding us of a point in astronomy, which is, that the longer the days are the farther off is the sun, and yet the more fierce.*

What it would be to read the pleadings of a Khmer king to one of the Ann Boleyns who must have existed in the Angkorian court.

The root authority of the Khmer epigraphy profession remains the eight-volume *Inscriptions du Cambodge* which the French scholar George Coedès published serially starting in 1937. The books contain his translations of one thousand five inscriptions and commentary on them.

In the same way that the musicologist Ludwig Ritter von Kochel brought order to the jumble of works that Mozart left behind, assigning a 'K' (for Kochel) number to every one, Coedès assigned a 'K' (for 'Khmer') number to each of the writings he analysed. Sadashiva's he designated as K 235. Inscriptions that survived with only a few words legible he classified as 'graffiti.'

Turning the pages of Coedès' books in the domed Main Reading Room of the Library of Congress, I knew I was handling a remarkable life's labour. Coedès not only translated each inscription, but, working at a time before computers, he cross-referenced them manually. Using charts he created, I could look up every temple name and find out which inscriptions originated there. I could look up every mentioned place or personal name (except those of slaves) and find out in which inscriptions it occurred.

Coedès' volumes are in French. That is another heritage of colonialism – Cambodians who want to read the full collection of messages their forebears left must learn a foreign language. But that is slowly changing. Some of the texts are being translated into modern Cambodian. And as part of a linguistic revival movement in Phnom Penh, a corps of educated Cambodians is learning Old Khmer, sometimes just for the satisfaction of it, doing language drills on laptop computers. This opens the door for them to read a good part of the ancient culture's record in the original.

In the meantime inscription experts continue to meet in academic conferences, to publish, to argue, sometimes over big points, sometimes over things as small as the meaning of a single word. Issues considered settled half a century ago by the great names of Khmer epigraphy are re-opened, new translations are done to correct perceived errors in earlier ones.

But there is still pioneering work to be done, because a number of Khmer inscriptions remain unpublished. And there is no end of things that might be newly deduced from the ones already accessible. Work continues, for instance, to try to understand the size of various units of measurement that the stones repeatedly mention.

Scholars will always listen to the 'whisperings' of the stones but the things are being subjected increasingly to modern computer analysis as well. In this approach, the information on each one is treated as a data set to be correlated with sets from other stones. Does the stone have a date? Where was it found? Does it mention a king? The information is entered with extensive keyboard work. Then database software can sort and sift to give answers on myriad questions or at least hints in the direction of the answer. It's not simple deduction, because researchers must be sure not to conclude too much from data that is hardly complete or fully accurate. Many stones are not dated, for instance, leaving scholars to deduce a date, sometimes accurately, sometimes not. Moreover, by arbitrary forces some stones survived and some didn't. A challenge for computer analysts is to filter out distortions that might result from lack of access to every stone the Khmers ever carved.

In a 2009 doctoral thesis for the University of Sydney, Eileen Lustig analysed data from 979 inscriptions dating from the 6th to mid-14th centuries, producing extensive charts and graphs. Among a host of conclusions, she found that inscriptions created for or mentioning a king tended to be clustered close to the capital Angkor. Within twenty-five kilometres of the Bayon temple in Angkor, they outnumbered non-royal inscriptions. But further out, the reverse became true. That would suggest that the king's authority decreased with increasing distance from the palace. Likewise, she analysed how changes over time in goods cited in large-scale barter transactions hint at growing sophistication in the underlying economy. Early inscriptions, for instance, stress payment in rice and textiles, whereas in later centuries animals and manufactured metal objects such as bowls and jewellery become more common.

As these debates continue, the Khmer corpus is gradually going on-line, following the lead of most every form of the world's information, to become available for viewing on computer screens in any country in the world. But another way to see inscriptions will always be the old-fashioned way, seeking them out 'in the wild.' At Banteay Chhmar, a huge 12th century temple in northwestern Cambodia, a restoration worker led me and a fellow visitor over great fields of fallen stone to a door-frame inscription. I looked, I photographed, I didn't touch. I can't read Sanskrit or Old Khmer, so I was left with feelings something like those that Henri Mouhot experienced in 1860. I was in the presence of something marvellous, 'a sealed book for want of an interpreter.' Happily that book has now been opened.

Brahmins at Angkor Wat.

Chapter VIII – Sadashiva's Testament

Praise be to Shiva!
Whose nature is proclaimed wordlessly yet thunderously
By the subtle soul-life of his body,
Which reaches everywhere
And quickens the senses of all living beings.

Thus opens the Sdok Kok Thom inscription, in Sanskrit verse rendered here in a translation published by University of Hawaii scholar Chhany Sak-Humphry with assistance from Philip N. Jenner. The temple was dedicated to Shiva, so the text begins with him and continues the adulation in the next three stanzas. Then things turn from heaven to earth.

There was once a sovereign of the world
Whose feet were clasped by all kings,
Whose part it was
To cause the hearts of men to unfold as lotuses,
Who dispelled all gloom,
And who by reason of his splendour was named Udayaditya.

This is the king reigning at the time the inscription was created, around 1052 AD. This man who dispelled all gloom has a name that means 'rising sun.' The clasping of feet is a classic Khmer metaphor for submission – the foot in that society, as in modern-day Cambodia, was the most profane part of the body, the head the holiest.

The next stanzas declare that Udayaditya had the full set of kingly virtues.

Quick to recognize forbidden women,
He would look upon another's wife unlustfully or as poison.
Yet did he enjoy in other ways
The ever sensual pleasures of those Wives of Duty:
Glory, Faith, Compassion, and Steadfastness...

That is to say, those four virtues were to him as beguiling as forbidden women might be to lesser men.

In battle he bore a sword red with the blood
Of enemy kings it had slain,
Which cast a dazzling light in all directions...

It flows on in a similar vein. Then, in stanza 45, the man who is in many ways the main character of this tale makes his entrance. We are informed that the king,

> *had a guru commanding high respect for his understanding:*
> *The celebrated Holy Jayendravarman,*
> *Born of a high-ranking family of irreproachable name.*

This is Sadashiva, identified by the honorific name that the king gave him some time before the inscription was composed. In terms of non-martial virtues, it seems, the king had some competition from the holy man.

> *He was the storehouse of that wealth which is Dharma...*
> *He was the ocean of that river which is propriety.*

> *His eyes were drawn to good conduct, not to the flesh*
> *For he was devoid of all thoughts of Love.*
> *Merit to be gained was what excited him,*
> *Not sound or other objects of the senses.*

Then the narrative jumps back two and half centuries to the very beginnings of the empire, about the year 800 AD, the time of its first king, Jayavarman II.

Jayavarman II ascended a mountain and there declared independence from foreign control, we are told. He founded a capital and eventually died there. Three reigns later, around the year 900, the story continues, a king moved the capital to the Angkor area and built a great temple there. Later the capital was moved again to a provincial city, before returning to Angkor. And after the year 1000, we get glimpses of civil unrest – temples have been desecrated, the stone informs us, their slaves scattered.

These key political events are recounted, and yet the inscription was not written as an imperial history. It is first and foremost a family saga, the tale of how for two and a half centuries this family of Brahmins served a succession of kings, twelve in all. Like in an historical novel, the reader learns of the times as backdrop to what the characters are experiencing. Indeed, whenever a major event occurs, it seems that some member of the Brahmin family is on the scene, helping, directing, advising, facilitating, whether it's the 'illustrious' Isanamurti, the 'noble-minded' Shivasrama, or Shivacarya 'of blessed aptitudes.' It's almost like the Forrest Gump story.

This is what puts this inscription in a class of its own: in a grand narrative, it recounts a lengthy stretch of the empire's run, roughly the first half. It provides a royal genealogy, confirming and expanding upon information found in other inscriptions. It provides a chronological framework for the court's movement between three successive capitals. It details a key religious ritual of kings. And it provides a unique portrait of a single family and its rise to become one of the wealthiest, most powerful and land-rich in the realm.

Getting a grasp of its countless nuances took decades. After Aymonier published his translation in 1901, the scholar Louis Finot came out with a version in 1915. Coedès, author of the eight-volume set of inscriptions, and Pierre Dupont gave a joint rendering in 1943. In more recent times, the Venerable Pang Khat and Long Seam created translations in modern Cambodian. The Thai Fine Arts Department did one in Thai. English versions have been published by Adhir Chakravarti, Chhany Sak-Humphry and Kamaleswar Bhattacharya. No doubt other translations will follow.

Angkor Wat in 1980, all but deserted. These local children were carrying fishing traps.

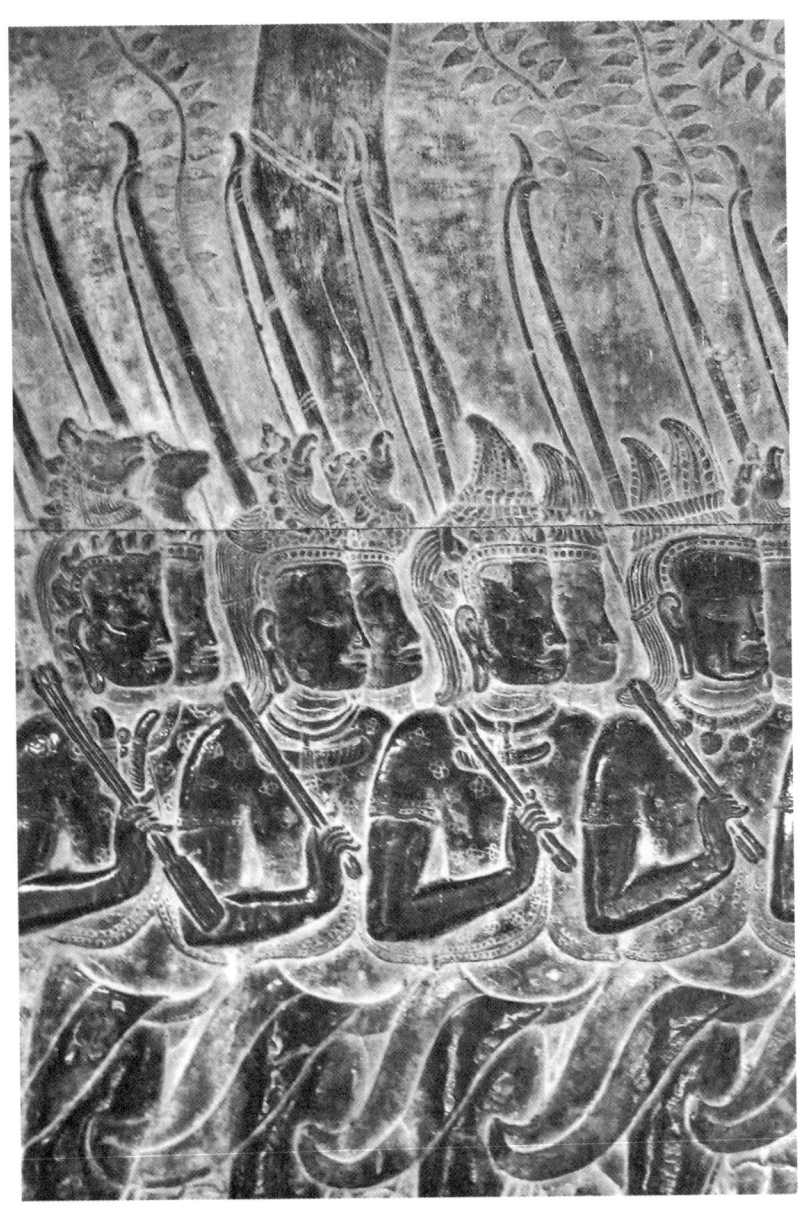

Khmer soldiers on the march at Angkor Wat.

Chapter IX – The Great Conqueror

George Washington, Attaturk, Romulus and Remus.

When Jayavarman II finally gets his due, people around the world will think of him in the company of names like those, history's great founding figures. He will become a part of basic cultural literacy.

He is the prince who around the year 800 created what we know today as the Khmer Empire. He is not myth. Yet getting a grasp of the man is difficult. No image of him is known to exist. No state temple that he built has been identified. We have no inscription authored in his name during his reign, no Chinese traveller's account of his court, no clear understanding of whether he brought on true centralised rule or rather opened the door to it happening later on. But we do have Sadashiva's stone, which tells us a lot of what we know about the man.

To get one obvious question out of the way, if he was the founder, why does he have a 'II' after his name? The reason flows from the fact that he did not step from a vacuum. The Southeast Asia into which he was born in the 8th century was already a thriving, civilised place of centuries-old mini-states, each with a rich heritage of culture, trade and expansionist longings. Historians have identified an earlier Jayavarman as ruler of one of those smaller realms and tagged him with the 'I'. The kings themselves did not use numbers in their names.

The state religion of those principalities was Hinduism, which had evolved on the Indian subcontinent in the fog of prehistory. Westerners often think of it as a faith of many, many gods. That is true, but it is also true that these gods are all expressions of different characteristics of a great monotheistic Godhead, whom the faithful know as the starting and end of everything, an unchanging, infinite being, ultimately indescribable in human language. It is through the Godhead that the eternal cycle of creation proceeds, carried out by the most important three gods of the pantheon that lies below: Brahma, the Creator, Vishnu the Preserver, Shiva the Destroyer. Lesser gods represent lesser aspects of divinity, all the way down to gods that have relatively small powers and are known and worshipped only in a single village.

There is no record of how Hinduism and its attendant practices and institutions came to Southeast Asia. Historians generally rule out military conquest and point instead to benevolent transmission by missionaries or traders. They must have brought along architects as well – anyone who has visited southern India can see the resemblance between its ancient temples and the Khmers'. What is clear is that sometime in the first centuries of the Common Era, the faith took hold among the kings and queens of Southeast Asia and indeed became the very basis of their rule. When I look at the bas reliefs with which the Khmers depicted scenes from Hindu mythology, the expression 'more Irish than the Irish' comes to mind. It is almost as if the Southeast Asian Hindus, by creating some of the world's most spectacular religious art, were determined to demonstrate that their grasp of the faith, their devotion, was every bit as strong as that of the priests back in its Indian homeland.

This is not to say that everyone was Hindu. By and large, villagers appear to have kept to their traditional animism, the worship of spirits. These deities could live anywhere – in a large shade tree, in a stream, in a mountain. Many were friendly, local, familiar. Others were not. All had to be propitiated with right ritual and right behaviour. This religion carried on in large part separate from Hinduism. Just as villagers dared not approach their kings, they dared not address prayers, directly at least, to their kings' gods.

This abiding animism points to one of the biggest continuing issues of debate among historians concerning this period – were these Southeast Asian cultures largely transplanted Indian cultures, or were they essentially indigenous ones with Hinduism grafted on top? Expressed another way, is a Khmer image of Vishnu really the Indian Vishnu? Or is it a traditional god with a new name and sculpted form, but remaining unchanged in its underlying spiritual essence? In recent decades, scholarship has tended toward the view that the indigenous ways were much stronger than previously recognised.

In these early times, Chinese who had travelled to the region wrote of a kingdom called Funan located around the Mekong River delta. Archaeological digs suggest that its main port was a site in present-day Vietnam known as Oc Eo, where jewellery, amulets, cymbals and an elaborate canal system have been found. The Chinese visitors gave lively but sometimes odd and contradictory reports about the people of this place. Funanese men were 'malicious and cunning.' Justice was through trial-by-ordeal, in which suspects were thrown into the water to sink or float. Boats had bows and sterns like the heads and tails of a fish. There were Brahmin priests who 'practice piety ceaselessly by day and by night.' For the most part the Chinese describe a unified state, along the lines of the centralised model they know from home. Modern historians are more likely to call Funan a collection of small competing states rubbing up against each other.

Around the 6th century, Funan disappears from the travellers' accounts. We hear instead of a kingdom called Chenla. By now, the local people are leaving behind quite another written record, stone inscriptions. We get names of kings – among them that first Jayavarman – and hints of palace machinations. There is said to be a split between north and south Chenla. And Chenla's people give us another invaluable historical record by putting up stone buildings that survived into modern times. All in all, we get a much richer view of the evolving civilisation. A Khmer ethnic identity is starting to firm up. But its people are not yet politically unified. They are constantly taking up sword and spear against each other. And other Indian-influenced states in the region appear to be trying to assert sovereignty over them. Military pressure comes from Champa, based in what is today central and southern Vietnam. Perhaps pressure comes too from the Hindu states centred in the islands that will become Indonesia.

We have now arrived at the time of the young Jayavarman II, the late decades of the 8th century.

There is no clear understanding of where Jayavarman was born and grew up and what brought on his quest to unify the Khmer principalities. But certainly his name is appropriate for the historical role he would play: *Jaya* is drawn from a Sanskrit root that means victory.

The sum of the inscriptional evidence suggests a birth of royal blood in southeast Cambodia and a years-long campaign toward power. It combined military conquest and peaceful tactics such as his marriage to a princess of another Khmer line. We can imagine Jayavarman II, chest bright with gold jewellery, gold headdress covering his hair, arriving at city after city atop his elephant, throngs of spearmen and archers at his command. During this time, he and a son may have fought not just against fellow Khmers but against Champa.

Eventually he and his forces reached the Angkor area. Just west of present-day Siem Reap, he set up court in a city named Hariharalaya in honour of Harihara, a god who melds Vishnu and Shiva (in sculpture, this deity is divided straight down the middle). This was to be the first of three capitals of the empire.

Sadashiva picks up the story. Historians note that he was writing a full two and a half centuries after the fact and caution that over that distance, the king might be seen as partially enveloped in the mists of legend. Still, the Sdok Kok Thom account remains the most detailed we have of this king and some of its facts are confirmed by other inscriptions.

In the following excerpts, Sadashiva refers to Jayavarman II by his posthumous name Paramesvara and tells us that at his side in this first capital was his chaplain, first of the Brahmin line of Sdok Kok Thom, a priest named Shivakaivalya.

> *While His Majesty Paramesvara reigned in the royal city of Hariharalaya, the August Shivakaivalya dwelt there as well.*

Then it describes a series of royal relocations.

> *When His Majesty founded the royal city of Amarendrapura, the August Shivakaivalya took up residence there as well and served him....When His Majesty left Amarendrapura to reign on Mount Mahendra, the August Shivakaivalya likewise went and took up residence there, serving His Majesty as before.*

Why so much moving around? The inscription offers no explanation. But a ready theory is that Jayavarman, like many great conquerors, had overextended himself. Princes whom he thought he had subjugated had begun rebelling against him after his departure from their districts. Jayavarman was now being chased out of supposedly secure locations one after the other. In this view, Mount Mahendra was the last stop on an emergency retreat, with king and entourage seeking a defensible stronghold in increasingly hostile territory. He needed some kind of bold and spectacular gesture to turn things around.

The priest's account suggests that to that end he employed not military force but an appeal to Khmer identity against foreigners who claimed the right to rule them.

The inscription now introduces another Brahmin, a man named Hiranyadama, who seems not to be of the Sdok Kok Thom line. 'Proficient in the lore of magic power,' he came from another city in response to a call from Jayavarman II, 'to perform a sublime rite' that would release the Khmer realm from foreign control. This priest 'respectfully exhibited before this king a magic power possessed of no other.'

So, a rite that amounted to a Declaration of Independence was carried out. Jayavarman II was no doubt a deeply religious man; he would have believed in the visiting Brahmin's powers. But in a strictly political sense, he was giving a message to his domestic rivals: Line up behind me. By Heaven's grace, we are now free of the foreigners. You can look forward to a new era of pride for the Khmer people, united under a single leader.

What was the foreign power? The inscription says 'Java.' At least that is how the word has long been translated. It also says that before his unification campaign, Jayavarman 'came from Java.' With those words began a hunt that continues to this day. Some call it a wild goose chase.

There is of course the island of Java, which at the time was the seat of another Indian-influenced state. Early French scholars could not resist the temptation to merge the priest's mentions of Java with a tale of uncertain veracity, said to have originated with an Arab merchant long after the Sdok Kok Thom stone was created. One day sometime in the 700s, it seems, a certain 'maharajah' heard that a young Khmer ruler had expressed a desire to see the maharajah's head on a platter. Outraged, the maharajah assembled a thousand boats and sailed to the Khmer capital. There he seized the startled Khmer ruler and lectured him: 'My victory will serve as a lesson to your successors; no one will be tempted to undertake a task above his power nor desire more than the share given to him by destiny.' With that lesson delivered, it was the Khmer's head that was placed on a platter. The maharajah sailed home, having urged the Khmers to this time put a wise man on the throne.

Surely, said those early scholars, surely this maharajah's realm was Java, and when he went home surely he took with him a Khmer prince as a hostage. And surely that prince was the future Jayavarman II! There arose stories of the founder-to-be living tragically as a captive in a foreign court in Java, perhaps with his family, learning the religion and arts of Java's civilisation but all the time yearning for his subjugated homeland. Then one day he is allowed to return. And once on the soil of his homeland, he unifies his people and ascends a mountain to declare independence.

Warrior atop chariot, Banteay Chhmar.

Later examination of language throws into question whether Sadashiva said Java at all. The historian Michael Vickery, for instance, has suggested that the word on the stone might in fact be meant as *'chvea'*, as the Khmers called the people of Champa, the state located to the east. And there is evidence from other sources of Jayavarman II having fought the Chams. Yet another theory is that the word did in fact refer to the island, but that it was the inscriptional shorthand of the time for any place under the influence of the state based on Java. That could have meant parts of the Southeast Asian mainland to the west of the Khmers' territory.

Among inscription experts, the Java word is today somewhat radioactive. Some make a point of saying they have no opinion on what it means.

Whoever the foreigners were, their yoke was declared cast off. Enough Khmer princes fell in line to allow Jayavarman to descend from his mountain redoubt and take up residence again in Hariharalaya. His faithful chaplain Shivakaivalya went with him, the inscription says, and died there before the end of his lord's reign. Jayavarman died in the city too. Whether he left behind a true state in any modern sense and how big is unclear. But he certainly firmed up the notion that Khmers should live under the rule of a single king. His many successors, expanding the frontiers and establishing something resembling political centralisation, would in their own inscriptions cite him and his great declaration atop Mount Mahendra as the source of their right to rule.

With the death of Jayavarman, Sadashiva continues the story of family members' service in the Khmer court forward for two and a half centuries of the empire. We learn that the royal court remained in Hariharalaya for two more reigns, then moved to a new city built a day's walk to the northwest. This place, today the location of Angkor Wat, the Bayon and a host of other temples, became the main locus of the empire's government and religion and is the area most visited by tourists today.

Later, the priest recounts, the court relocated to a city he calls Chok Gargyar, known in modern times as Koh Ker, a hilly place that lies several hours' drive northeast of Angkor and has its own fascinating set of ruins. After two reigns there, a new king and his Brahmin assistant of the time came back to Angkor. As the story moves toward its conclusion in the 11th century, Sadashiva makes allusions to civil war and unrest – soldiers on the move and the destruction of various family properties are noted – but the priest offers no explanation for this upheaval.

The inscription's royal genealogy is not a chart or list in the modern sense. Rather, it must be extracted from the narrative. But that is not so hard: Kings make their appearances in chronological sequence, sometimes with information as to whose sons they were. In total, twelve kings are described.[1]

Early examination of the inscription turned up something puzzling concerning their names. The Sanskrit section gives a succession of twelve monarchs whose names ended in *varman*. The Old Khmer section listed eleven kings with names ending in such suffixes as *svara*, *loka* and *pada*, and one king with a name ending in *varman*. In most other ways, the information in the two sections is largely analogous. The events and sequence of reigns are recounted in the same way, the names of the gurus serving at those times are the same. The kings in the two lists seem to be the same people.

Why then the different names? Back in France, working with early information supplied by Aymonier, the Sanskrit scholar Abel Bergaigne took a stab at answering. He matched each name in the Sanskrit section with its apparent counterpart in the Old Khmer section. To him, the most likely explanation was that the names in the Old Khmer section were surnames of some kind. But he noted the one exception to the pattern – the name Udayadityavarman was used in both sections. He was the king reigning at the time of the inscription's composition, the one monarch in the list who was still alive. 'One is naturally led to ask oneself,' Bergaigne wrote, 'if the names ending in loka and pada had been reserved for kings who had died.'

He was on the right track. Subsequent research established that upon death each Khmer king received a posthumous name that described his status in heaven. Jayavarman II became Paramesvara ('Supreme Lord'), for instance, his son Jayavarman III became Vishnuloka ('In the Realm of Vishnu'). In Sanskrit texts, it was common to use the king's living name, in Old Khmer ones, his posthumous one.

So it was that Sadashiva's chronicle became a priceless tool in efforts to piece together Khmer royal history.

---

[1] In at least two cases, Sadashiva chooses to be diplomatically silent. He makes no mention of a king who is widely recognised as the first to bear the name Udayadityavarman. Around 1000 AD, after a short reign, this man was swept aside by one of the empire's greatest kings, Suryavarman I, in a civil war. Nor does the inscription say anything about another man whom Suryavarman defeated, Jayaviravarman. Some historians consider him to have held the throne briefly. Others doubt he was ever really king.

Linga placed in central sanctuary of Phnom Rung Temple.
Courtesy of Stephen A. Murphy.

Chapter X – The God King

I first saw Angkor in 1969, as a college student. At the time, my family was living in Bangkok, where my father was UNICEF director, and I was visiting from the United States for summer break. One day, my mother and I boarded a plane for the short flight to the then largely peaceful Cambodia.

My fascination dates to that visit. Angkor Wat, the gates of Angkor Thom city, the Bayon, Ta Keo – we saw them all, our jaws dropping, as happens with most first-timers. It was at this time that I first heard the tale of the aggrieved maharajah, told by a fellow Western tourist who'd already gotten the Angkor bug. We encountered him one day while taking a break on some upper-level steps of a largely deserted Angkor Wat. It was like that in those times. You could practically have the world's largest religious edifice to yourself.

It was also on this trip that I first heard that Khmer kings were divine. This was the very foundation of the Khmer political system, we tourists were told. It went beyond European notions of rule by heaven's authority. Khmer monarchs were deities walking among mortals, bringing order and purpose to life on earth. They were 'god-kings.' The term turned up everywhere in 1969, and it's the same today, taken home by every Angkor visitor. It's there in coffee table books on sale in Siem Reap, in tour guides' lectures at temple gates, in restaurant conversation after a day at the monuments. In 1998, a film was released documenting the life of the country's most important royal of present times. Its title, to no surprise: *'The Last God King: Sihanouk of Cambodia.'* And when word came in 2004 that Sihanouk's son, Sihamoni, would take his father's place on the throne, *The Times* newspaper of Britain reported that Sihamoni would become 'the revered god-king of this nation of 13 million people.' A Google search for the words 'god-king Cambodia' generated 114,000 returns.

Certainly the term seemed to explain a lot concerning ancient history. The king depicted in the bas reliefs of Angkor Wat, Suryavarman II (see illustration page 27), is hardly distinguishable from gods shown elsewhere in the grand stone pageant, which runs for close to 800 metres inside columned galleries. The king wears the similar jewellery across his chest and on his arms. Atop his head is a similar diadem and overhead are similar parasols, which were (and are) emblems of rank. And having a god in the palace would help explain how the ancient peoples summoned the tremendous sacrifice that went into building the temples.

Years later I learned that the whole god-king phenomenon originated with a few lines in Sadashiva's text.

Let us return to Mount Mahendra, to which the Brahmin Hiranyadama has been summoned. He has performed the rite that freed the Khmers from foreign control. And now the king presses the priest to share his knowledge.

At the king's behest, this Brahmin imparted magic power
And its practices to this chaplain,
Whose pure heart, for the increase of his power
Was intent upon the good.

That officiating priest was the king's own Shivakaivalya, first of the Sdok Kok Thom line.

As if by magic means,
This Brahmin taught him the treatises
Entitled Sirascheda, Vinasikha, Sammoha and Nayottara,
Those four faces of Tumburu.

This Brahmin, having distilled the essence
Of these treatises with understanding and experience in mysteries,
Established for the world's prosperity
The magic rites that bear the name of devaraja.

Devaraja. In Sanskrit, 'deva' means god, 'raja' means king. Literally: God-king.

In his 1901 commentary on the text, Aymonier wasn't sure what to make of this word. He suggested that it could mean the gods Indra or Shiva. Or the king himself.

It was that last interpretation that was seized upon in the popular mind and remains firmly embedded there today. Indeed, this is the one word of Sadashiva's testament that, in the god-king translation, has made it into the world's common language. The visiting priest, in this view, had performed a ceremony that transformed Jayavarman II into a god. And the secrets of that rite, disclosed to the court's own holy man, were available to his descendents to make all subsequent Khmer kings divine as well.

Certainly it was mastery – of magic, of secret Hindu texts and ritual – that gave Brahmins their privileged place in Angkorian society. The stone goes to some lengths to inform us of the qualifications of Sadashiva, 'whose noble heart was ever Shiva's throne.'

> *Tirelessly reciting the text of treatises to be learned,*
> *he then imparted them to others...*
> *The fully opened lotus of his heart was fragrant with the*
> *Sabdartha and other treatises...*
> *He knew music; he had learned the arts (mechanics, astronomy,*
> *medicine and others); he was master of ritual.*

Today we can see Brahmins in those bas reliefs at Angkor Wat. Each man sports the priesthood's distinctive pointed whiskers and cylindrical hair-do. Several of them sit, arms crossed, in the presence of Suryavarman II. Another, standing and looking away from the king, directs two more who are carrying jars that might seem to contain holy draughts. Elsewhere on the bas relief, Brahmins are shown in procession behind the ark of the sacred fire, shouldering their master in a covered palanquin.

This elite survives through to modern times, part of that huge cultural inheritance that shapes contemporary society in Southeast Asia. The Cambodian and Thai royal households continue to include Brahmin gurus who oversee important ceremonies, such as an annual ploughing rite that helps make fields productive. Other Brahmins are available to carry out special rites for ordinary people, such as blessing a stone-laying ceremony at the start of a building's construction, with offerings that may include a cooked pig's head, flowers and incense sticks.

Procession of Brahmins at Angkor Wat.

In Sadashiva's era, big Brahmin clans could be found in many parts of the empire. Boys were trained as future priests by their fathers (in the Angkor Wat bas relief, a boy with the distinctive headdress if not the whiskers walks in procession with his elders). Girls could not grow up to become priests or hold top positions but were sometimes given special titles and recognised in inscriptions as persons of unusual piety. Still, it was not an entirely male-dominated system. Females had a special standing in determining which man got the hereditary posts. The bloodline for priests, as for kings, was generally maternal, that is, what often mattered in succession was who your mother was rather than who your father was. When a Brahmin died, he would often be replaced not by his son, but by the son of his sister, so as to preserve the maternal blood. In fact, that was how Sadashiva came to be head of the great family.

Perhaps the Brahmins' most important spiritual function was maintaining the *lingas*.

In modern Cambodia and Thailand, the *linga* is considered a phallic emblem of Shiva's divine attributes. Some Hindus, however, will tell you there is nothing phallic about it – prudish Christian missionaries in colonial India, they say, could think of no other explanation. What the *linga* really is, in this view, is a holy mountain in miniature, or a representation of a column of fire, a form that Shiva once took.

Lingas come in many forms and sizes. They are shafts, semi-globes and a twenty-metre temple tower which is said to be the tallest *linga* in India. They might be made of stone, wood, crystal, blocks of ice or flowers.

The typical *linga* of Angkorian times was a stone shaft set upright on a stone base that is today often called its female counterpart. Just as there was a hierarchy of gods, so there was a hierarchy of *lingas*. The holiest was installed at the peak of a mountain temple, to be tended only by senior priests and royalty, with lesser *lingas* enshrined on lower levels of the temple. Many of the rituals appear to have focused on the pouring of holy water or perhaps sanctified milk over the *linga*, with the liquid being collected at the *linga's* base for re-use in lesser rites. On special occasions, the king came in procession to his state temple to do the honours himself at the supreme *linga*, communing with a stone with which he often shared a common name.

Though it was fixed in the popular mind that the *devaraja* was a deified king, many scholars rejected that interpretation early on. But what was it, then? This single word has generated more pages of scholarly exegesis, more history conference debates than any other in the Khmer experience.

If the term did not mean 'god king' perhaps it meant something closer to 'king god,' as in king of the gods. Aymonier had considered that. One variation of this theory has it that the *devaraja* was a *roi abtrait*, an abstract king. The contemporary scholar Claude Jacques, meanwhile, suggests that the *devaraja* was a supreme spirit, 'sovereign of the many spirits whose protection was implored in time of need, then as now, throughout the country of the Khmers.'

Or perhaps the *devaraja* was a set of ritual practices – indeed the initial reference in the text is to 'the magic rites that bear the name of *devaraja*.'

Over time many experts have focused on the idea that whatever the *devaraja* was in theological terms, it was also a very important *thing*. The inscription seemed to be saying that the *devaraja* was forever being tended to, ritually honoured and moved around, following the king, not on his day-to-day comings and goings, but on his longer-term relocations from palace to palace, capital to capital.

One of Sadashiva's Sanskrit verses says this of certain bygone family members:

> *Residing in the royal city, these excellent learned men of high intelligence,*
> *Worthy of the homage and the company of kings,*
> *Thus celebrated punctually, strictly, zealously,*
> *The daily service to the* devaraja *and none other.*

And a passage in Old Khmer, using that language's counterpart term, Sovereign High Lord of the World, appears to be referring to an important object.

> *When His Majesty Parameshvara returned to reign in Hariharalaya, the Sovereign High Lord of the World was brought with him.*

Coedès believed that the *devaraja* must be a *linga*, the supreme one at the top of the reigning king's state temple – and indeed, one passage does say that a member of the priestly line set up a *linga* when the capital was moved around the year 900.

But other scholars have argued that the object was something else. In a paper published in 1974, the historian Hermann Kulke noted that many Indian temples today have a fixed primary *linga* and a secondary object that is moved around to stand in for the *linga* on certain days of the holy calendar. This object may be not a *linga* but an image. He cited a temple at Bhubaneswar, Orissa, and its four-armed, figure of Shiva standing about fifty centimetres high.

In reading Sadashiva's account carefully, and factoring in mentions of the *devaraja* in later inscriptions, Kulke concluded that the term likely referred to some kind of bronze depiction of Shiva, definitely not the main *linga*. The image was probably kept not at the state temple but in the palace, close to the king. When the king relocated to a new palace or capital, the image was escorted there and put in a new place of honour. It functioned as a 'palladium,' he believes, a repository of divineness whose preservation would ensure the preservation of king and empire at large.

In the following passage, the High Lord of Earth is the king, while Sovereign High Lord of the World is the image.

> *The location of the Sovereign High Lord of the World changed with the royal city in which the High Lord of Earth resided, and was taken with him. It is this divinity that safeguarded the realm from that time on.*

Kulke deduced that there was just a single *devaraja* image, the one consecrated atop Mount Mahendra for Jayavarman II, and that this image had passed from king to king through the ages, tended all the while by the same priestly family. There was no divinity rite for kings, Kulke believed. They were viewed as human beings, though hardly ordinary ones. Countless inscriptions talk about the king's 'inner self' residing in the *linga*. But it is one thing for a king and god to have a special association and another to be one and the same.

But where the *devaraja* is concerned, debate never quite comes to a rest. In 2001 Hiram W. Woodward Jr. put forward the view that the *devaraja* was a thing but not an image. Rather, after analysing linguistic terms and religious practice, he suggested it might be the hearth in which burned the royal fire, a key symbol of kingly authority. He noted the bas relief at Angkor in which Brahmins are shown walking in procession just behind an ark that contains the fire vessel. Significantly, he noted, the Brahmins are marked royal *hotar*, the same title that Sadashiva gave for members of his line. 'The close association of *hotar* and fire is clearly stated at Angkor Wat,' he wrote.

If the *devaraja* was a physical thing, there would also have been a very specific and exclusive set of ceremonies to be conducted in its presence. Sadashiva says several times that his family was accorded exclusive rights for these rites by the founding king and the visiting Brahmin Hiranyadama.

> *May no others but an ascetic of this maternal line and gifted with learning and vigour be priests of this worship!*

Indeed, this appears to have been a big part of why the priest wrote at such length on this subject: he was making a declaration of a royally accorded monopoly function at the palace.

So just what might the family's speciality rituals have been? Some of the Hindu texts that the inscription cites as having been passed on atop Mount Mahendra have been identified. The Vinasikha is one, existing in a copy on palm leaf in Nepal. In more than three hundred forty verses, it gives detailed instruction for such tasks as creating a *mandala*, the holy diagram of Hindu mysticism, all the way down to the colours of lotuses it must have.

Because their standing depended in part upon possession of secret knowledge, Sadashiva's family probably went to great trouble to keep the precise rites secret.

It succeeded. For the most part, we are still guessing.

Ark containing the royal fire is carried in procession in an Angkor Wat bas relief.

Beng Mealea temple.

Chapter XI – Dates Confused

From just a few of Sadashiva's sentences sprang one of the longest and most embarrassing foul-ups in modern efforts to understand Angkor.

Since the time of Henri Mouhot, the French had longed to understand the sequence of construction of the major temples. Determining the progression would create a framework of time – there would no longer be just static ruins in the jungle, there would be history. But for close to fifty years, the best French minds, Aymonier's among them, insisted on misreading what now seem like fairly clear pointers that the priest left behind. The savants missed the mark by as much as three centuries concerning the age of the Bayon, Angkor Thom city, Beng Mealea and many other of the prime Angkorian monuments.

The words in question concerned the kings' repeated relocations of the seat of government.

Sadashiva's account had imperial founder Jayavarman II establishing himself atop Mount Mahendra. When that passage was translated, there began a hunt for the mountain – none in Cambodia still bore that Sanskrit name, which means 'Great Indra.' The search proceeded with the same impulsiveness and willingness to jump to conclusions that coloured efforts to locate Atlantis, Troy and Mount Arafat.

Aymonier joined in the hunt. He did his homework, noting that another inscription said that waters of Mount Mahendra flowed down to Angkor. That, he reasoned, pointed to the low mountain range that had come to be called Kulen, located in a sandstone-rich range to the north of Angkor. It was the site of many of the temples' quarries. Aymonier climbed Kulen. But at its upper reaches, he found nothing of note – just 'four or five impoverished hamlets.' He was convinced that wherever this Mount Mahendra was, it must have a large temple. So he cast his eye toward Beng Mealea, the enormous sandstone temple that lies not far from the base of the mountain he'd climbed. To Aymonier, it seemed a fitting legacy for a man of Jayavarman II's stature – 'a marvel of sober grace, of nobility and regularity, in which the rooms are larger than in other Cambodian edifices.' It was true, he conceded, that Beng Mealea was on a plain, but couldn't the rocky ground on which it stood be viewed as an extension of the rocky mountains nearby?

Aymonier duly noted that the question was still open, that there were arguments to the contrary. But the great man had spoken. In many minds, Beng Mealea was now the temple of Jayavarman II.

Stories in Stone

From the mountain, Sadashiva had said, the king moved back to the capital Hariharalaya. That place was easily and accurately identified early on. Today it's known as Roluos, located about ten kilometres east of Siem Reap, the provincial capital where most visitors to Angkor stay. There is nothing there that is firmly attributed to Jayavarman II or to his successor. But the empire's third king, Indravarman, built or improved major temples and reservoirs there, such as the pyramidal Bakong temple.

Indravarman's son, Yasovarman took over as the fourth king. He put a major brick temple, Lolei, on an island in a reservoir his father had built. But he also got to thinking of moving the capital. Perhaps he had a religious vision, perhaps he wanted farmers to have more water than they found in the somewhat dry fields around Hariharalaya. Perhaps he merely wanted to leave behind his father's city and build with a clean slate. So, on land about fifteen kilometres to the northwest, he broke ground around the year 900 AD.

Sadashiva, using Yasovarman's posthumous name, picks up the story with the transfer of the *devaraja* from the old capital. We can picture an elaborate procession moving along those fifteen kilometres, with ringing bells and drums, the holy object held aloft.

Gate of the Dead, Angkor Thom City.

Of course, a forebear of the Sdok Kok Thom abbot was involved. In this case it was Vamashiva, who in addition to his palace duties headed up a religious retreat called Shivasrama.

> When His Majesty Paramishivaloka founded the royal city of Yasodharapura, he brought the Sovereign High Lord of the World from Hariharalaya and installed it in the new royal city. When His Majesty raised the Central Mountain, Vamashiva, High Lord of the Shivasrama, set up a holy linga in its centre.

To return to the inscription, a question naturally arose among the early scholars: what was this 'Central Mountain' that the king had raised?

Many declared it must be the Bayon, the sandstone temple that today is one of Angkor's biggest draws, a sublime creation that blurs the distinction between architecture and sculpture, enchanting visitors with its mammoth stone faces. Certainly, with so many of its stones lying scattered on the ground, so many of its walls buckling, it must date to the city's earliest days. Concerning the word 'mountain,' the experts reasoned that it was metaphorical – the Bayon's great main tower symbolised a holy peak. But the word 'central' seemed loaded with literal meaning. The Bayon lay at the precise centre of the near perfect square established by the more than three-kilometre-long walls and moats of Angkor Thom city.

Now, if the Bayon was the Central Mountain, then everything built in its style would also be the initial creations of the new capital and date to about the year 900. These would include the walled city Angkor Thom and its five gates and a collection of huge temples outside the city's gates.

This dating was as good as truth for many decades. Whenever evidence to the contrary surfaced, the experts struggled to explain it away.

For instance, in some of these supposedly early temples archaeologists found inscriptions bearing the name of Jayavarman VII, the empire's last great king, who ruled until about 1220, three centuries after Yasovarman moved the capital. Discovery of the name of a king in a temple was often the gold standard of evidence concerning who had built it. But no, said the experts, not in this case – these inscriptions in question were all carved on free-standing stones that could have been added to the temples centuries after their construction.

The first real challenge to the view came from Philippe Stern, an art historian in Paris. He'd never been to Cambodia but at his desk

Phnom Bakheng temple.

he'd studied in detail the flood of photos and diagrams that were circulating among academics in France.

In a book that he published in 1927, he argued that there was no real basis for the accepted dating of the Bayon. 'Where does it rest? On a single inscription, found far from the capital, and on the position of the Bayon in the city of Angkor.' That far-off inscription was the Sdok Kok Thom stone – and had Stern known what we know now, he would have said 'on a misreading of a single inscription.'

But his main point was that it just didn't make sense that the Bayon-style monuments could be so radically different in style from the temples of the first capital, Hariharalaya, yet follow them so soon. Architectural evolution needed to take its time. The Hariharalaya temples, he noted, were built of brick, red in colour. 'The sudden appearance, at the moment of the foundation of Angkor, of the Bayon and other great monuments, all in grey,' he said, would have been stunning. He found similar implausibly fast evolution in such things as floor plan, collonettes and lintels. Surely, he said, the Bayon and related buildings must date to much later than previously thought, perhaps 1050.

That got discussion going. In an article the following year, the great inscription specialist George Coedès congratulated Stern for having the nerve to question dogma, but said he wasn't right on his new timing estimates. The Bayon monuments went up around the year 1200, Coedès boldly declared, a full three centuries later than conventional wisdom.[1] They were not the first but the last great buildings of the capital, the work of that final great king, Jayavarman VII.

He based this assertion in large part on long hours spent with his beloved words from the past. He noted that one stone, found at the northwest corner of Angkor Thom's walls, appeared to mark a ceremony in which Jayavarman VII took possession of the city. The text contained flowery verse likening the city to a young bride, 'burning with desire,' being given in marriage to Jayavarman VII. Coedès asked, would such an allusion have been made if Angkor Thom had already been there for centuries? Wouldn't a city compared to a young bride more logically be something new that this king had just created?

And he cited another stone, this one inside a Bayon-style temple, that lavished praise on Jayavarman VII's mother, calling her among other things the 'Mother of the Buddhas.' Coedès found it impossible that the king would have re-used a predecessor's temple to honour his mother in this way. He could only have built it himself.

In later years, archaeological digs and more study of inscriptions confirmed that Coedès got the dating right. The tumbled-down state of the Bayon-style group of constructions, it turned out, was due not to age, but to haphazard foundations that were a common engineering short-cut in the empire's last great construction boom. But the original question remained unanswered: what was the 'Central Mountain' that Sadashiva mentioned?

It is hard to understand how so many smart people resisted for so long what now seems obvious.

Just a few hundred metres to the south of Angkor Thom city is a steep hill called Phnom Bakheng. If not tall enough to qualify as a real mountain, it at least exacted a good sweat from me when I made the twenty-minute climb in January 2009. At its top is a very large temple, known today, like the hill, as Phnom Bakheng. A tiered pyramid, the temple is one of the few in Angkor that, dare it be said, is not particularly beautiful. Imposing, yes. But its unknown architect lacked something. Henri Mouhot noted as much after his own climb up the hill: 'Genius was not in proportion.'

---

[1] Coedès laid out his views in a 1928 article entitled *Études Cambodgiennes*. In the article, he muses over the confusion that would result if future archaeologists dated Paris' Arc de Triomphe, completed in 1833, to the time of King Louis XIV, who reigned from 1643 to 1715.

Perhaps this temple didn't fit romantic notions among the early experts that Angkor's most dazzling architecture must date to its first glorious years. Phnom Bakheng seems never to have received serious consideration in the search for the mountain that the Brahmin mentioned. Even from Philippe Stern. He correctly deduced that it dated to Yasovarman's reign, but he designated a temple inside Angkor Thom city, the Phimeanakas, as the Central Mountain.

It took a scholar named Victor Goloubew to finally steer things in the right direction. In a series of articles in the 1930s, he proposed that Phnom Bakheng must be the Central Mountain. His conclusion was in part drawn from old-style techniques such as style analysis and digs that had turned up remnants of gates and symmetrically arranged pools at the foot of the hill. But more than that, Goloubew cited what he'd learned through a remarkable new method of archaeological survey. In August 1932, two French military planes had been put at his disposal, and Goloubew went aloft twice, peering down on the monuments and the surrounding terrain through remarkably clear air. He was getting heaven's view of Angkor. A lieutenant took photographs from about four hundred metres. The following January, two French airmen based in Vietnam flew back and forth over the ancient capital, making an additional one hundred ninety-two photographic plates.

When you looked from this new perspective, Goloubew announced, you could see remnants of a mammoth rectangular moat and river system measuring roughly five by six kilometres, with Phnom Bakheng right at the *central* point. The southwest quadrant of this system, a great L-shaped structure, was plain as day. Missing portions, he theorised, must have been obliterated by the construction of later kings or incorporated into their own water management projects.

From Phnom Bakheng, the king would have looked out over a vast city contained within these moats. *La Ville de Yaçovarman*, he called it. The City of Yasovarman.

Sceptics dubbed it 'Goloupura' (*pura* means city in Sanskrit). But Goloubew stuck with the theory, investing his reputation and years of research. He visited Angkor repeatedly in the 1930s. The builders of Angkor Thom city had placed explanatory inscription stones at the corners of its moats; Goloubew went by elephant-back to that southwest corner of his water system in hopes of finding something similar. He did not.

Extensive work of later decades confirmed that yes, Phnom Bakheng was the Central Mountain of Sadashiva's text – today no

Angkor from space. The large square at the top centre right is Angkor Thom city. The L-shaped structure that so intrigued Victor Goloubew is visible at the lower centre of the image. Phnom Bakheng shows as a small light mark just outside the lower wall of Angkor Thom and slightly to the left of its centre point. Photo courtesy of U.S./Japan ASTER Science Team.

one questions that. But not so Goloubew's idea that it was enclosed by such a huge rectangle of water. Archaeologists working on the ground have largely failed to find the missing parts of Goloubew's great rectangle system. There is no denying that there's that huge L-shaped dike system to the southwest (it is known today by the archaeological designation CP807), but digs suggest that it was built centuries later than Phnom Bakheng. If not to enclose the temple, why is it there? No one has yet come up with a convincing explanation for such an enormous feat of engineering, so large that in satellite photos it continues to stand out as one of Angkor's most visible features.

So the 'mountain' of King Yasovarman was no metaphor. In fact, this monarch built atop the real thing wherever he could. To the east of Phnom Bakheng is the hill known as Phnom Bok. Yasovarman placed a three-towered temple at its summit. To the south is the hill known as Phnom Krom, which becomes largely an island when the waters of the Tonle Sap lake make their annual advance. The temple that Yasovarman constructed atop it is an ultimate symbolic tableau of a natural holy mountain surrounded by a natural Sea of Creation. Standing atop Phnom Bakheng, Yasovarman would have been able to see the two other mountaintops on which he'd built, as I could the day I climbed the hill.

The savants had all read Henri Mouhot, but concerning Phnom Bakheng they might have saved themselves some trouble by taking his words more seriously. The man who by his own admission had no formal expertise in archaeology sensed that this temple must date to very early in the capital's history. Noting its aesthetic shortcomings and stone that crumbled to the touch, he surmised that it was a 'prelude to civilisation.'

Though the identity of Phnom Bakheng is today firmly established, the place hardly gets the respect it deserves. In the age

The brick towers of Lolei temple, viewed from the northwest.

of global tourism, it has become in effect a set of stone bleachers. Late every afternoon, just before sunset, crowds troop up the hill, on foot or by elephant at twenty dollars a ride. Then they climb the temple's steps to the plaza-like upper tier, which becomes as jammed as the Woodstock rock festival. From it, people get a priceless view of Angkor Wat as the day's final sun rays bath its stones. Then they throng back down the hill as darkness closes in. Most never realise that they have stood in a spot that in its day was the centre of the universe.

Happily, a major program to protect and shore up Phnom Bakheng is underway, bringing together skills and money from organisations that include the World Monuments Fund, Cambodia's Apsara Authority and the U.S. State Department. Controls are being imposed on the many sets of feet. When I visited, ancient laterite steps that ascend the hill on three sides had been closed off and visitors were channelled up a spiral trail that loops around the slopes. Wooden footbridges carry people harmlessly across the crumbling steps. But many many feet still erode the steps of the temple itself, which were built very steep, because the ascent to heaven is never easy.

Beng Mealea's provenance was finally nailed down as well. The mammoth complex is now confirmed as unrelated to founding king Jayavarman II. It is roughly contemporary with Angkor Wat, placing it around the year 1150, about two and a half centuries later than the first monarch's reign. The two temples have many stylistic similarities. Perhaps Beng Mealea was a great architect's dry run for innovations, such as galleries, that were used to great effect at the better-known temple.

And Mount Mahendra? All bets are that Aymonier climbed the right mountain. It's just that Jayavarman II didn't build anything up there, at least anything huge (quite a number of old but smallish temples are now known to exist in the mountain's upper slopes). To this day, no surviving monument anywhere has been firmly connected to the founding king. Perhaps he was too busy building an empire to have time to build *things*.

Outside of inner eastern *gopura*, 2009.

Chapter XII – The Brahmin Landlords

In the American frontier of the 19th century, powerful families amassed huge spreads of land, using it to generate wealth and political influence. As the Khmer Empire expanded, Sadashiva's clan did the same, becoming a Southeast Asian version of American television's Cartwright family of Ponderosa fame. By the time the priest sat down to write history, his clan was one of the biggest land owners in the realm.

It had pulled off this feat by being useful in a vision shared by virtually every Khmer king: conquer as much territory as possible, then clear and develop it. Kings smiled if temples rose on virgin land, rice fields replaced forest. Roads and bridges were built to tie the empire together, becoming busy with merchants, oxcarts and soldiers. In the Khmer mind, jungles were places to be feared, the haunt of menacing spirits, carnivorous animals and disturbing jumble. Always preferred were the straight lines of temple walls and reservoir banks, orderly rows of farmers wading across a flooded paddy planting rice seedlings.

As court insiders, Sadashiva and his forbears appear to have been among the first to know when land was coming open. And the Brahmins did not sit back and await royal gifts. King after king was lobbied for new tracts, to the point that I can imagine exasperation in the throne room when the latest petition arrived.

Land was on the Brahmin's mind to the point that his text in places might be called a collection of real estate deeds. He documents repeated land grants and how these locales were dutifully settled and civilised by family members. Certainly many other inscriptions document rights to land, but the detail and expanse of this one is remarkable. So many towns and districts are listed – the French translator Louis Finot counted a total of eighty-one place names – so many grants described, that I had to read these sections many times before things started to fit together in my mind.

In theory, all land in the empire belonged to the king.[1] But, as happened often in medieval Europe, he doled out tracts to ranking people who had won particular favour. Or, prominent families might purchase it, paying in barter goods. Rights to land could be revoked, when dynasties changed, perhaps, or disloyalty or ingratitude was suspected. But all signs are that once high-

---

[1] The French found this system still to be in existence when they made Cambodia a protectorate in 1863.

ranking people put down stakes on a patch of land, they as good as owned it, though on specific conditions, typically laid out in an inscription. For instance, if the king provided land to establish a new temple and support priests in lives of prayer, an important issue was to sort out to whom the resulting religious merit would accrue. Treating it in effect as a form of income being generated, inscriptions often state that the merit will flow back to the king personally. The texts sometimes also state that the new temple will be immune from certain types of real-world taxes. It can begin to look like a quid pro quo agreement, with the king's collection of merit cancelling out his right to collect taxes.

Big land owners everywhere generate resentment among their neighbours, and there are quite a few Khmer inscriptions that suggest that rights were often contested. After making private purchases, some buyers petitioned the king to confirm that the land was indeed theirs. A change of monarch could result in a flurry of requests to the capital that he formally reconfirm holdings that his predecessor had recognised.

Reading between the lines in Sadashiva's text, we can detect concerns that the family's rights were facing challenges that must be countered squarely.

The clan began to amass its land even before Jayavarman II took the throne as the first king. The stone tells us that the line's founder, Shivakaivalya, the man who was with the founder atop Mount Mahendra, had already received land from a prince, head of one of the pre-Angkorian mini-states. Once Jayavarman II was established in power, his priest asked for more land from him, and got some. On it he created a commune that he named Bhavalaya, settling some family members there and installing a *linga*. The great range on which Sdok Kok Thom would eventually stand was starting to take shape.

Close to a century after Bhavalaya's founding, Vamashiva, the family patriarch in the time of King Yasovarman, met with another priest who told of 'ravaged lands,' apparently near Bhavalaya. Vamashiva petitioned the king for these lands, was granted them, and set up a new district called Bhadrapattana. One of the priest's disciples was appointed by the king as a sort of general contractor and surveyor, and was told to take two assistants to the land and set up an image. This man 'laid out the district and carried out works on the site of the said image, in particular erecting the temple, the enclosing wall and pinnacle.' Vamashiva asked the king to incorporate the clan's old Bhavalaya district and three other districts into Bhadrapattana. This was done; the range had again been successfully expanded. A younger brother of Vamashiva added further to the holdings through his own petition to the king. The brothers brought three of their nieces from the Bhavalaya commune and settled them on new land.

In the first part of the 11th century, civil war engulfed parts of the empire. A prince who would take the name Suryavarman I fought his way toward the capital, declaring himself king even before the many years of fighting ended in victory for him.

The clan's lands suffered mightily during this period. Sadashiva limits his description to a few details – perhaps it was too unpleasant a thing to commit to stone – but he mentions that images at multiple family holdings were desecrated two years after Suryavarman I became king. Badhrapattana, for instance, was abandoned by its priests and slaves; the wilds closed in over its stones. When peace was restored, the family patriarch of the time began work to repair these places, but died before the job was finished. This job passed to his nephew, son of his sister – Sadashiva.

At five sites, the new patriarch carried out extensive reconstruction, building pinnacles, walls and dams, while providing the newly reopened temples with slaves and 'all manner of costly things.' Badhrapattana received a *linga*, two images and a pinnacle surrounded by a laterite wall. Slaves and 'a channel and a pool there for the region's prosperity' were also provided.

One of the repaired temples was in Bhavalaya, the old seat granted by Jayavarman II. This place had lain abandoned for so many years that ownership was apparently up for grabs. Perhaps squatters had moved in. To defend the family's rights, Sadashiva made a filing to the king, pointing out how the family had originally acquired the land and asking that ownership be reconfirmed. The king concurred.

But like so many of his forebears, Sadashiva wanted entirely new lands as well. Some of it he got by buying it, paying with barter goods. Other land came under family control in the old way, through petitions to the king. One such acquisition shows how different inscription stones often confirm each other. The Sdok Kok Thom stele talks of the king giving a certain ravaged district over to Sadashiva. In that district, about fifty kilometres away from the Brahmin's temple seat, archaeologists have found another stone that also reports the transaction, saying that the old owners had no sons or grandsons to take over and so the property was merged with a district owned by Sadashiva's family.

His account of yet another acquisition reads like a modern title search, painstakingly tracing ownership history lest someone later

The outer wall, with the outer eastern *gopura* at right, Sdok Kok Thom, 2009.

challenge the purchase. This tract, he says, had been bought from a holy order in the year 972 by a priest and his son, both foreigners, for two taels of gold, 320 garments, a quantity of cloth, four goats, four sacred cows and twelve water buffaloes. Following the death of the priest-father, the son petitioned the king to transfer the land to Sadashiva, the inscription says, giving no reason why, on condition that the land's slaves be held back for two additional years.

Of course, the long narrative finally arrives at the construction of Sdok Kok Thom, referring to it by its Sanskrit name Bhadraniketana. It calls Sadashiva by one of his honorary names, Jayendravarman, and applies to him yet another honorific, 'dust of the feet,' an allusion to even the dust on those appendages being holy.

> *His Majesty ordered a minister to go and lay out the commune named Bhadraniketana on land in Bhadrapattana belonging to the new Dust of the Feet My Holy High Lord Sri Jayendravarman, to set up on his behalf a holy linga two cubits in height, and to give four hundred male and female slaves to the image. Sri Jayendravarman [thereafter] erected a stone temple with pinnacle, dug a reservoir, built dikes, and laid out fields and gardens.*

We can see all of those things today. And it was a stunningly beautiful temple then, as now.

> *Whoso views this ideal abode, foremost on earth,*
> *Or merely hears it spoken of,*
> *His mind is at rest, his soul is sanctified.*

The boundaries of its land are specified: on the southeast it runs the equivalent of about 215 metres to the marker of a commune called Kadamba; on the northwest it goes about eleven hundred metres to the marker of Lmun commune, abutting also on a river. I can imagine surveyors reporting to the priest after having paced off the distances or measured them by rope.

Nearing its end, the inscription lists surrounding villages that support the new temple by sending teams of workers on a waning moon-waxing moon schedule.

The inscription's final words in Old Khmer wrap up the labour roll call.

Settlement of Pin Khla: 1 male overseer and his party of 4 males and 13 females.

In the Sanskrit portion, the priest closes with words that would often be ignored in the centuries ahead.

He who by word, thought or deed
Shall harm what is Shiva's – be it land,
gold, silver, slaves or other things,
Shall undergo atonement in the two worlds.

With that, Sadashiva's clan vanishes from history. It is never heard from again.

Ancient levy (background) extends north from Sdok Kok Thom, 2009.

Image of Luang Poh Boon Tham, located outside inner eastern *gopura*, Sdok Kok Thom, 1979.

Chapter XIII – The Resident Spirit

Sdok Kok Thom was at a time unknown abandoned to the jungle. But it never ceased to be a holy place. As the years passed, the deserted temple continued to inspire reverence among Cambodians and later Thais who made their homes in the area, farming the paddies that the ancients had laid out, raising cattle, hunting small animals. As the 20th century dawned, the stone temple in the forest was known in local Thai villages as the abode of a great spirit, Chao Poh Sisuto, Lord Father Sisuto.[1]

There could be no question – ancient temples always had a spirit, and this particular spirit frequently signalled its presence. More than once, people passing close by heard strange music coming from the overgrown courtyard. They smelled the smells of cooking. And there was the great fireball that one night flew up from the temple, arcing high across the air.

Every so often, the spirit possessed someone and through this medium addressed the local people. Announcing its name, it laid down how it expected to be treated. One big rule: No hunting in the forest around the temple. It also banned cutting the local timber or bringing cattle to graze on nearby grass. These prohibitions were passed from parents to children, down through the generations, and people learned that there was a price for defying them. No matter how good you were with your rifle, if you tried to shoot squirrels around the temple your bullets would miss. Other punishments were severe. There was the child who fell from a tree after an infraction and died, the woodcutter who opened a terrible gash in his hand with his own axe. Cattle sometimes were found mysteriously dead, their necks broken. A few people who'd defied the spirit went out of their minds.

But the spirit had another side. People came to know that Chao Poh Sisuto was in some ways like a wealthy gentleman who owns a big spread of land in the county. If you were polite, if you showed respect and homage, he would allow you things that were supposed to be forbidden. Steering clear of him was perhaps the safest thing to do, but if for some reason you had to go to the temple or the

---

[1] This chapter is based largely on interviews in 2009 and 2010 with about a dozen older residents of Nong Samet and Koke Soong, the Thai communities closest to the temple. Recollections differed, details and dates were sometimes in conflict, but by and large people told the same story. I have drawn on information from the interviews to create an account that I believe reflects the realities of the time.

surrounding forest, it was very important to ask permission first. Kneel at the inner eastern gate. Burn some incense and offer some fruit. And whatever you do, don't use bad language in the vicinity. Everyone knew of people who'd made these kinds of gestures, then chopped their wood or shot their birds and come home unharmed.

With proper homage, the spirit could even be prevailed upon to actively intervene for you. If you were about to go off on a trip, for instance, it was a good idea to first go and say prayers and burn incense, because Chao Poh Sisuto could grant you protection along the road, just as in the human world a prince might give a loyal subject a letter of protection to show along the way to anyone who might interfere.

In the adjacent villages today, most everyone beyond a certain age uses idyllic terms to describe the temple in the old days – beautiful, stones largely intact, full of trees, quiet and peaceful, its moats always filled with water. But with perhaps just a hint of trepidation in their voices. Generally they went only in the company of friends. Going alone would have been too frightening.

Word of the holiness of Sdok Kok Thom spread beyond the district and over the years there came a succession of what Thais call *phra thudong,* wandering monks. These men of the robes, part of a revival movement that began around the turn of the 20th century, believed that enlightenment was to be found not in the comforts of a modern temple, but on the road as an ascetic, in the forest, as the Lord Buddha himself did. Meditate alone, surrounded by nature. If a place of special spiritual energies could be found, all the better. While ordinary people might do well to avoid such places, true holy people would be welcomed. The resident spirits would recognise their sincerity, their virtue and perhaps even hope to absorb some of it themselves.

Sometime in the 1950s or 60s, there appeared such a monk at Sdok Kok Thom. Known as Luang Poh Boon Tham, Holy Father of Merit and Law, he was from Surin, a Thai province in the northeast where many people spoke Khmer, a hold-over from the area's history as part of the great empire. He established himself at the temple, meditating right in the sanctuary chamber where the Shiva-*linga* had stood, focus of the temple's cosmic energies.

Villagers were impressed with his piety. Many went to the temple to hear his sermons and receive water blessings. Some received amulets said to have special powers due to association with him and the temple. People with illness sometimes came hoping the monk might cure them, as other wandering monks had been known to do. While some villagers saw Luang Poh Boon Tham simply as a golden-hearted, pious monk, others felt that he had true supernatural powers.

At some point, it was decided that, ascetic or not, the monk should have a proper place to live. So holy quarters were built for him just outside the now buckling laterite walls of Sdok Kok Thom. To mark their consecration, a huge festival was thrown in the forest, right at the temple. Villagers arrived by oxcart, by foot, to take part in merit-making ceremonies. Elephants, holy beasts in the Hindu and Buddhist tradition, were brought in to walk in procession around the temple. After darkness fell, people enjoyed the standard entertainment genre of Thai temple festivals, a Chinese sword-fighting movie, projected onto a screen hung up for the occasion. How noisy it must have been – probably there was a gasoline generator on the scene too. But the resident spirit would likely have been accepting. This tumult was taking place to honour a truly holy man.

Memories differ on how it was that the monk eventually left. By one account, he was joined in residence at the temple by another monk, a local man, who died tragically. While meditating, the man was bitten by a snake. He was taken to a hospital in Aranyaprathet, the district town about thirty kilometres to the southwest. There he died. After that, the temple seemed not as good a place for a forest monk.

Other accounts cite effects of the early stages of conflict in Cambodia. In the 1960s, insurrection was brewing against the government of Prince Sihanouk in Phnom Penh. Remote border areas of the type where the temple stood often drew rebels seeking haven from government attacks. There may have been suggestions that the monk leave the temple for his own safety, or even threats to that effect.

So for whatever reason Luang Poh Boon Tham ended his stay of many years. But the local villagers did not lose him altogether. They still had his teachings in their hearts. And, following a Thai Buddhist tradition, they had a sculptor from a northeastern province cast a life-size image of him, hands together in his lap, legs folded, eyes closed, in the classic pose of meditation. Its colour was black, for reasons that local people differ on: the monk was a dark-skinned man, black can be a holy colour.

The image was placed outside the inner east *gopura* of the temple, framed by a false window. There it welcomed anyone who approached in piety and burned a stick of incense.

As late as around 1970, a single colonette remained in a window of Sdok Kok Thom's northeast library and a *naga* head remained at an upper corner. By 1979, both were gone. Courtesy of Muang Boran Data Center.

Chapter XIV – Pillage

Thai folk belief has a theme of hidden treasure in holy places – golden Buddhas encased inside ordinary-looking plaster ones, jewellery stashed in temple walls or buried in the soil below. In some cases, there's clear factual basis for this. The Golden Buddha of Wat Traimit in Bangkok, for instance, is believed to have been cast around the 13th century, but at some point was covered over with plaster, likely to hide its true nature in a time of war or civil unrest. The secret was only revealed in the 1950s when the image was being transferred from one temple to another and a plaster chip fell off.

In the villages around Sdok Kok Thom, not a few people believed that there was treasure at the temple. By some accounts, Chao Poh Sisuto had in the distant past been a flesh-and-blood human being who buried a cache of fabulous valuables in or around the temple. The spirit was haunting the place in order to safeguard these things pending reincarnation into the world of human beings.

Around 1940, a monk from some far-away district took up residence in the temple, behaving in the manner of a forest monk in search of quietude and meditative peace. 'Monk Long Nails,' this man was called, for the length of his fingernails. After a while, the locals got to wondering about him: was he meditating, or was he looking for Chao Poh Sisuto's treasure? And was he *finding* it? Stories circulated that the monk had been seen covertly burying things in the forest near the temple.

Distrust reached the point that villagers filed a formal complaint with government officials in Aranyaprathet. The District Officer came to the scene, a considerable journey in days of dirt roads and forest paths, and conducted an investigation. Leung Gert-thong, a retired farmer, was a student at the time. He saw with his own eyes the event that the village was all abuzz about: Monk Long Nails, at the village school, sitting alongside the ranking village official. In the end the District Officer found no proof of wrongdoing. The monk returned to the temple, but after a while he disappeared. For a long time after that, bold villagers went into the forest and dug near the temple, looking for any treasure that the priest might have stashed. Nothing he'd left was ever found.

But after a while, treasure *was* found at the temple. Only it didn't gleam and sparkle.

For many years, local people had lived in ignorance of the cash value of the temple's cornucopia of sculpture. A farmer, working a field near the temple, one day unearthed a human-sized statue of a god, missing an arm but otherwise in good condition. He brought it home and leaned it up against his house as a curiosity. It seems never to have occurred to him to try to sell it.

But gradually, merchants of the world's growing underground trade in antiquities made their way to the temple's district. Looking back, it's surprising it took so long. Collectors as near as Bangkok and as far away as New York and London had long been willing to pay big money for the artistic creations of Khmer antiquity, and a clandestine network of dealers, stout-armed village men and venal officials had come together to meet that demand.

Around 1960, a Bangkok antiquities dealer arrived in the district with a proposition for local villagers. If you bring out carved stone from your temple in the forest, I'll pay you good money for it. Sometimes payment was in barter – a sack of rice, perhaps. The understanding that the man gave was that foreigners would be the ultimate buyers.

According to Kancharup Champasook, a Nong Samet resident who was a guide at the temple before his death in 2009, Sdok Kok Thom was at this point perhaps eighty to ninety percent intact. The main sanctuary rose tall and almost complete, despite the stone-splitting powers of tropical vegetation. The sculpture included six free-standing stone lions, each about a metre high, arrayed in pairs along the ceremonial avenue to the main sanctuary's *linga* chamber.

Partial confirmation comes from two photos taken in 1959 by J.J. Boeles (see page 22), at the time the head of the Siam Society, Thailand's foremost academic organisation devoted to culture and history. They show the eastern door of the northeast library from different angles. Fallen rubble is visible through the door, but on the library's exterior, hardly a stone is out of place. An elaborate lintel with a seated deity in the centre tops the door. Above are two high-balancing pediments with *nagas* undulating down either side.

Kancharup was about twenty when the dealer came calling. He was told he was too young for what was to follow, but on some days he went in and watched. Teams of about twenty men carried out the dangerous, exhausting work. Over time, five of the six lions came out. Pediments were knocked down for their carving. Lintels, important structural elements, were crudely ripped out, bringing stones above them tumbling down. The loot was carried to Nong Samet village. From there word was passed to the dealer in Bangkok, who sent hirelings to pick up the new haul. The villagers received the Thai currency equivalent of $25 for a lion, $50 for a carved lintel and $500 for a high-quality statue.

Pillage

Stone is removed from the eastern gallery for carving into holy images, 1984. Courtesy of Cameron Macauley.

After a while, the easy pickings were gone. But there were still things visible high up the central tower that the dealer would buy, if only they could be got at. So dynamite was obtained. *Boom! Boom!* Whole sections of the main sanctuary came crashing down; stones flew left and right, coming to rest far from the tower. And I had assumed in 1979 that the destruction I saw, the broken stones lying about, was the work of nature.

In addition to the theft, a more benign form of removal had been underway. A number of the temple's carved stone posts were taken by oxcart to the Buddhist temple in the village of Koke Soong a couple of kilometres away. There they were set up in a ring around the main sanctuary of the village's Buddhist temple, performing the same spiritual function they always had, the delimiting of holy ground. The village's Buddhist faithful worshipped within their embrace. I believe that we should thank the people who organised this removal – their motives were good and they no doubt saved objects that otherwise would have disappeared forever into the world's underground art trade.

It's unclear how long the dismantling continued. Photographs likely taken in the late 1960s or early 1970s show the main sanctuary gutted, but a wonderful lintel and floral carving still in place over the false western door to the inner courtyard.[1] By the time I first saw the

---

[1] These photos were taken by a team conducting research for construction of The Ancient City (*Muang Boran*), a giant historical park that opened outside Bangkok in 1972. The park features replicas of many of the great ancient buildings of Thailand, among them Sdok Kok Thom's inner courtyard and sanctuary, beautifully rendered in roughly half scale. Negatives of black and white photos of the real thing were retrieved from the archives of the affiliated Muang Boran Data Center, but had no notation about date (see pages 46 & 100).

temple in 1979, that was gone too – there was now just a giant scar in the wall, with stones scattered helter-skelter underfoot. Another of the pictures shows a section of pediment still in place atop the northeast library that was in such good shape in 1959, a single collonette still in a window. Not so when I first visited.

So how did villagers go from revering the temple to ripping it apart? It should be noted that the for-profit looting seems to have been carried out by a small minority of people. For them the only motivation was money. The Bangkok dealer was dangling unimaginable sums before farmers who were among the poorest citizens of what was then a generally poor country. It was like the temptation of selling drugs in an American city. There are always people willing to accept big risks for big returns.

No doubt some of the men tried to make apologies to the spirit in advance, requesting understanding for their extreme need for money. Others tried to turn the tables and get tough with it. The dynamite was in part meant to frighten the spirit away. After each explosion, some of the men called out to it: Go away now! Get out! Still, many of the looters are said to have suffered tragedy later in life. Mental illness struck some, while the marriages and families of others were shattered. Kancharup figured he escaped this kind of retribution because all he did was watch.

According to other accounts, Chao Poh Sisuto was angered too by the removal of the stone posts to the Koke Soong temple. Their transport away by oxcart was accompanied by a huge storm, the wind blowing, the rain with an intensity that got people noticing.

Where is the missing stonework today?

In early 2010, I saw two of the stone posts at Koke Soong village's Buddhist temple. They lay on their sides in the shade of a tree as they awaited return to the temple at the behest of the Thai Fine Arts Department, which has jurisdiction over archaeological sites. Other posts had already been taken back. Local people say they are happy about that – the great stone temple, pride of the district, is being made complete again.

And at the Prachinburi province branch of Thailand's National Museum, on proud display in a second-floor gallery, I saw a fragment of a lintel from Sdok Kok Thom. It includes a *garuda* and part of the lovingly carved head and torso of a deity. Somehow the looters overlooked it. Art officials recovered it from the site, where it had stood over the main sanctuary's false west door.

As for the rest of it, I have no idea. I found no instance of a world museum displaying a piece that is labelled as coming from Sdok Kok Thom. Interpol has nothing on file about sculpture from

Sdok Kok Thom lintel at Prachinburi museum. Courtesy of Bandith Lewchaichan.

the temple and inquiries to people who know the art trade turned up nothing. But it's likely that Sdok Kok Thom sculpture labelled 'Khmer, Sandstone, 11th century' or something similarly ambiguous is today on display in world museums. Or in dens and living rooms in world capitals, tastefully illuminated by track lighting, owned by collectors who don't know how these particular trophies came to be on sale and know better than to ask. I can picture guests offering polite compliments, then looking back to glasses of wine.

Let's hope that one day Sdok Kok Thom will have the good fortune that blessed another Khmer temple in Thailand, Phnom Rung.

That story begins in the 1960s, around the time that the Bangkok art dealer was striking his pilferage deals in the villages. Over a main eastern entranceway at Phnom Rung was a lintel showing that very important scene of Vishnu in cosmic slumber, creating a new cycle of the universe. During restoration work, masons removed the lintel and set it aside. The lintel disappeared. After passing through a number of hands, it arrived at the Art Institute of Chicago in 1967. After some years, its display there became a major source of outrage among Thais. Protests were mounted outside the U.S. Embassy in Bangkok and outside the Chicago institute as well. The Thai government demanded the return of the stone; the institute responded that it had been acquired legitimately. Newspapers accounts of the time have U.S. officials anonymously pointing the finger at Thailand, suggesting that corruption there was to blame. Why, they asked, had someone been able to take such a thing out of the country in the first place? Eventually, the lintel was returned, arriving aboard a United Airlines flight in November 1988. It went on temporary display in Bangkok, drawing thousands of admirers.

Later it was put back in its original place, over that eastern door in the temple where Khmer masons installed it close to a millennium ago. It remains there today.

Phra Thinang Sivamok Piman as it stands today.
Courtesy of Paisarn Piemmattawat.

Chapter XV – The Stone's Fate

And what of the temple's most important artefact?

Happily, Sadashiva's gift to the ages was not there to be carted off for some foreign collector. But it had a tragic story of its own.

We back up to the year 1920. Luang Charn Nikom, a Siamese police captain, walks through the forest to Sdok Kok Thom, led by the abbot of the Buddhist temple in Koke Soong village. Local people tell the captain that about twenty years earlier the French sent some men and an elephant to drag the inscription stone away, presumably to neighbouring Cambodia. But for some reason they were unable to complete the task and left empty-handed. Was this an early for-profit art heist attempt or a well intentioned initiative to safeguard an important piece of history? The French were by this time far along on efforts to systematically survey the Angkorian heritage in Cambodia and preserve things that they deemed to be in danger.

Recollections of just when something happened a long time ago can be unreliable, so it is conceivable that the villagers were referring to Aymonier and team making their visit to the temple in 1883. Aymonier's writings say nothing of trying to take the stone, but certainly we know from his letters that he did take others and this one would have seemed quite a catch.

We have an account of the local people's words because the police captain sent his superiors a report which has survived. In it he also notes doing a quick survey of the temple. Reading his words in the original Thai gave me a whiff of the challenges the French faced in decoding the Khmer stones without a full knowledge of the language. Though I studied Thai for years, I never became as proficient as I might have. So as I went through the captain's report, I puzzled over nuance and meaning that the writer had or had not intended for specific words and phrases. The captain reported seeing the inscription stone but his description of where left me wondering: did it mean 'in front of the temple, to the north side.' That would suggest it had been moved outside from its original spot in the galleries' northeast corner. Or did it mean 'in the front of the temple, to the north side.' That could suggest it had stayed put.

But then I read further and grasped that clearly it wasn't in its original place. The policeman gave measurements: 'Its height from ground up is about three cubits. Its depth below the ground is a similar amount.' It was leaning, he noted. He was describing

A lesser known inscription from Sdok Kok Thom dating to 935 A.D., 65 cm. high, now kept in the National Musuem, Bangkok. Courtesy of Paisarn Piemmattawat.

a stone planted in the soil, not standing on a stone base in the temple's gallery, as Aymonier had found it.

So let me offer the following theory on the captain's modern-day inscription: the French team, whoever they were, wrestled the stone from its original perch and brought it outside the temple to prepare it for transport. It was too heavy, perhaps, and they ended up abandoning it there. Villagers later decided that so holy a thing, covered with the secret words of heaven, should not be left lying in the dirt. So they dug a hole, wrestled the base into it, then filled in soil to make the monolith stand upright again. Like the ancient Khmers, they scrimped on foundations. Rain water gradually undermined the stone. It began to lean.

Using some foolscap paper that happened to be at hand, the captain made a rubbing of the carved words and sent it up the chain of command along with his report, in which he stated that the stone was clearly something 'important.' He was trying to sound the alarm to protect it.

Certainly there were people in Bangkok open to such concerns. Siam, soon to rename itself Thailand, had by this period the glimmerings of a home-grown preservation movement. At its centre was Prince Damrong, a monumental figure in the country's modern cultural history. He was a son of King Mongkut, the 19th century monarch who set Siam on the path to modernisation. Damrong did not get the throne, but he got a long, illustrious career. He studied the ancient Indian language Pali. He helped establish the country's public school system. He wrote widely on events of previous reigns. And he took a close interest in the ancient Khmer monuments that lay within his country's borders, moving to protect them from thieves and decay.

In the case of Sdok Kok Thom, politics as well as preservation was in play. As the last independent nation in the region, Siam was feeling under siege. In 1893, French gunboats had sailed up the Chao Phraya River to Bangkok, exchanged fire with shore batteries, and trained cannon on the royal palace. Siam was forced to cede broad swathes of territory in Laos. In a 1904 treaty, the French had compelled Siam to agree to the return of vast areas of western Cambodia, including Siem Reap province, location of Angkor, where the Siamese flag had flown since annexation in the 18th century. In 1906, the Siamese and French sat down to negotiate the specifics of a new demarcation line for Siam and Cambodia. When they were done, the soil on which Sdok Kok Thom stood remained Siamese, the two sides agreed. But French Cambodia was just a short walk away, hardly a few hundred metres. Who could say whether the French might tomorrow force Siam to give up more territory and this time get the temple?

At some point in the 1920s, the Thai side took action. A Siamese conservation engineer who was returning overland from a course in Angkor stopped at the temple and organised the stele's transport to Bangkok for safekeeping in the National Museum.

This did not sit well with Étienne Aymonier, who was by now an aged man living back in France.

This 'marvel' of a stone, he complained in a footnote of a history book he published late in his life, belonged in the Louvre in Paris; instead it was in a museum in Bangkok. He essentially accused some of his countrymen of dereliction of duty for failing in the 1907 talks with the Siamese to route the border so as to include the

Inscriptions gallery at the National Museum Bangkok.
Courtesy of Paisarn Piemmattawat.

Stories in Stone

Phra Thinang Sivamok Piman as it stood before it was destroyed by fire. The photograph dates to the reign of King Rama VII (1925-1935). Courtesy of RBC.

temple. 'When Siam ceded to us so many of the celebrated ruins, not one negotiator of the treaty of 1907 thought to also reclaim the insignificant temple that sheltered that stele... Not one expert or man of science in Indochina, it appears, knew to remind one or the other that this ruin with its baroque and non-euphonic name, Sdok Kak Thom, was the humble box that contained this invaluable jewel.' This oversight happened, he complained, even though the stone was famous by this time 'among people other than I who brought it to light.'[1]

---

[1] In research, it's always frustrating to come across contradictory information in sources that otherwise seem reliable. For this reason, I was not able to determine exactly when the stone was moved to Bangkok. The Library of Congress catalog lists the book in which Aymonier aired his complaint as having been published in 1920, which would mean the transfer took place in that year or earlier. But the book itself gives no publication date. I suspect that the transfer took place considerably later than 1920, because Police Captain Luang Charn Nikom is known to have visited the site that year. And a brief item in a 1930 *Bulletin de l'École française d'Extrême-Orient* reports the removal in terms that suggest it was something quite recent. There is contradictory information too as to who caused the stone to be moved. Thai documents say that Prince Damrong ordered it; the BEFEO item depicts it as a result of long lobbying by George Coedès, who at that time was secretary general of the Royal Institute of Siam.

However Aymonier felt, the main French academic organisation concerned with Khmer antiquity, the L'École française d'Extrême-Orient, praised the move. In a brief item in its professional journal, it reported to readers that the stone was now in 'a shelter sure and definitive.'

In ensuing years, many other ancient inscription stones, Khmer and Siamese alike, were brought to Bangkok from archaeological sites around Thailand, for study and safekeeping. Among them was a second stone from Sdok Kok Thom, dating to 935 A.D., 115 years before Sadashiva's. It appears to have been associated with a temple that stood at the location before Sadashiva built the current one. As inscriptions go, the message is rather brief and undistinguished. Among other things, it states that parties assigned to look after rice and oil offered to the temple are forbidden to take them for use as their own and that those who oversee the shrine itself must not send its slaves to do other work.

The stele collection continued to grow. But then came the night of 9 November 1960.

Foreign tourists had gathered in the Silpakorn Theatre in central Bangkok to see some traditional Thai performance arts. The show finished at about 10 p.m. Shortly before midnight, a fire broke out in the theatre. The flames quickly spread, engulfing the theatre and jumping to the adjacent Phra Thinang Sivamok Piman Building, part of the National Museum. Consumed were shadow puppets, Thai musical instruments, antique cases (these wonderful gold-inlaid creations were collection items in their own right) and old writings. The loss would have been larger had not about fifty boy scouts been gathered nearby that night and gone bravely into the museum. They carried a number of very heavy cases out the door to safety.[2]

This was the building in which the stone was kept, and the scouts did not bring it out. Given its weight, it's hard to see how they could have.

As the fire continued to burn, the surface that Sadashiva's mason had engraved so lovingly nine hundred years earlier became warm, then hot, then near incandescent. The stone's internal structure gave way. One of the world's greatest historical records broke into countless fragments.

---

[2] This account is taken from the *Bangkok Post* of 10 November 1960.

Khmer Serei fighters take a break at Camp 007 in 1979. AK-47s were the fighters' standard weapons; sometimes they were turned on rival Khmer Serei groups.

Chapter XVI – Resistance Stronghold

It is 1979. A band of armed men is walking northeast at mid-day through rice fields and forests that lie along the border of Thailand and Cambodia. The sun shines strong through dry season cloudlessness. The fields are barren plots of cracked earth awaiting rain that is still months away; trees shed dead leaves that crackle beneath the men's feet.[1]

The fifteen men are members of a militia that calls itself the Black Eagles Movement, after a bird of prey that prowls the skies of Southeast Asia. Their group is one of many that have formed spontaneously, answering only to themselves, in the months since a Vietnamese invasion force overthrew the Khmer Rouge. Cambodians are rejoicing over the Maoist fanatics' downfall but not at what has followed. Soldiers from the country's historical enemy have settled in for a long occupation. They have installed a government that takes its orders from Hanoi. The foreign troops, wearing their standard-issue green pith helmets, stand guard at seemingly every bridge, every crossroads, every district office. Periodically they sweep swathes of countryside, seeking to wipe out the last resistance to their client government's rule. But not a few Cambodians remain determined to keep up the fight and so have come together as bands such as the Black Eagles. Equipped with just a few rifles and grenades, the 'Khmer Serei' or Free Khmer make the audacious claim that they will defeat the army that defeated the United States. They will establish an independent, non-communist, democratic Cambodia.

Thailand is watching the evolving conflict with concern, because Vietnam is also *its* historical enemy. For centuries Cambodia served as a buffer between the two countries; now Vietnam's soldiers have swallowed it up. So the Royal Thai Army has deployed troops in defensive positions just back from the border. On the other side, the Vietnamese are keeping a bit back too, apparently to avoid unintended clashes with the Thais. But who can say they won't get orders to push across the border, even to march on Bangkok?

---

[1] This chapter draws on interviews with the people who are quoted, books and my own memories, articles and photographs from the period. My collection of negatives and slides, stored for thirty-odd years in various boxes and drawers, yielded only one roll of black-and-white 35mm film of the temple, though I am certain that I took more, having always had a camera with me in those days. Interspersed in my photos of the temple are images of militia officers, an injured man eating, and a refugee boy minding a baby, all indications that the temple was indeed at the centre of the border crisis.

In between the two armies is a no-man's land measuring a few kilometres wide and hundreds long, running essentially the length of the common border. This zone has become a haven for Cambodian civilians who are fleeing war and food shortages in their towns and villages, and for that potpourri of anti-Vietnamese armed groups. Khmer Rouge remnant units that retreated and survived are the most disciplined and lethal of these. There are also guerrillas loyal to the country's former leader, Prince Sihanouk, to a former prime minister named Son Sann, and ad hoc bands such as the Black Eagles. Thailand variously supports or tolerates these groups in the belief that anyone who makes trouble for the Vietnamese is a friend for the moment.

Some members of the Black Eagles Movement have been staying at Camp 204, a collection of huts that refugees put up in 1979 next to a Thai border village called Non Mak Moon. But the fighters' commander has been feuding with 204's leader, who has a small army of his own. So after a month, the Black Eagles' members pack up their equipment and march north, heading for another border spot about eight kilometres away that has been attracting refugees.

One of these Black Eagles is a young former university student named Mour Ley, who spent the four years of Khmer Rouge rule in forced labour in the fields of western Cambodia. His group of fifteen, led by a local guide, reaches the new site and pitches camp. Several days later, he is told that there is something remarkable in the forest nearby. He and a comrade go look. It is an ancient stone temple, just like the ones at Angkor. It creates a feeling of soaring elation in Mour Ley. It seems to embody the nationhood for which he and his comrades are fighting. Mour Ley kneels and prays before the temple. 'It represented our soul, our heart,' he later recalls.

Thus began a new role, a new identity for Sadashiva's creation. For the next five years Sdok Kok Thom functioned as a rallying point for the Cambodian nationalist cause. For the first time in centuries, the temple was again the focus of a large population centre, as Camp 007 expanded rapidly. Through control of the temple and the conducting of public ceremonies at it, the succession of resistance factions that held sway in the camp sought to demonstrate legitimacy to Cambodians.

This is the period when I came to know the temple. In October 1979, when I first walked in from a Thai road, it seemed to me that there were already tens of thousands people in the camp. But that was just a guess. It is better just to say that there were multitudes. All I knew as I wandered through was that I was in a place that

Camp 007 was teeming with children, like these young residents of 1979. Smiles were common, despite the very difficult living conditions in the camp.

went on forever and was as teeming as any temple fair. Except here people wouldn't go home after dark. For now home was a spot claimed beneath a tree. The kitchen was a campfire, the toilet a plot off to the side dotted with faeces. Horrifying conditions, but most everyone seemed glad to be here. One sign of that joy was clothes. Black pyjama-like garments had been more or less a uniform in the labour camp that was Khmer Rouge Cambodia. Here the black things were cast aside and replaced with colourful fabrics that Thai villagers carried in on their backs and sold at outrageous mark-ups.

Many people left 007 as soon as they could for the greater safety and order of a camp that the Office of the UN High Commissioner for Refugees established in Thailand about fifteen kilometres back from the border. At this place, service in the Cambodian army that the Khmer Rouge defeated in 1975, a former job as a driver at a Western embassy – in short any kind of old connection with foreigners – might be parlayed into resettlement in the United States or some other country. But not everyone had such credentials. Many ended up settling in for the long term at 007. It wasn't on any map, but for a period it was one of the largest cities of Cambodians anywhere.

The commander of Moul Ley's group in the camp was a man named In Sakhan. In addition to the fighters, he was chief of one of many short-lived political organisations of this period of Cambodian history: the Angkor National Liberation Movement. With that name, he attempted to harness the ancient glories, as most every Cambodian political movement does. But he had an advantage, physical possession of one of those ancient glories. With Vietnamese soldiers occupying the temples of Angkor, not many other resistance leaders could match that claim.

A small child riding an oxcart at Camp 007.

In late 1979, In Sakhan led a lengthy ceremony at Sdok Kok Thom. He and about two hundred fighters and refugees gathered there one morning. Incense was burned, prayers were intoned – that people would remain safe, that peace would return, that the nation would be liberated. Following Buddhist tradition, they walked in procession around the temple, burning incense and repeating prayers at each of the collapsed corners of its courtyard. It was a spiritual but also a political act.

Refugees continued to arrive. One group that reached the camp around 1980 was a family of nine – mother, father and seven children. They had survived four years under the Khmer Rouge, then spent a month hiding in the forest as Vietnamese troops hunted down soldiers of the brutal movement. Later the family returned to its old house in Battambang province, only to find that there was no food or work there. So they made for the border.

It was a long, exhausting trip, along potholed roads patrolled by Vietnamese soldiers, then footpaths that traversed riceland. Hang Sobratsavyouth, then a 10-year-old boy, recalls the journey's end. 'I knelt with my mother at the Black Buddha.' He lit some incense, and said a silent prayer. To him the image, beckoning at the entrance of an ancient stone temple, signalled safety.

Technically speaking, it wasn't a Buddha. It was the life-sized image of the monk Luang Poh Boon Tham whose piety had so moved the local Thai villagers some years earlier. But what mattered now was what Cambodians thought the image was, the founder of the faith the Khmer Rouge had attempted to eradicate. The Lord Buddha was offering protection to the camp a short walk away. Countless Cambodians said prayers before the image that year, leaving behind a veritable forest of incense sticks. Sdok Kok Thom acquired a new name: the Temple of the Black Buddha.

But however safe they felt on having reached the camp, they soon found that they needed protection there as well, sometimes from fellow Cambodians. Despite rhetoric of devotion to the Khmer people and nation, resistance fighters frequently turned their guns on each other, right in the middle of this and other camps. Disputes were generally less about military strategy than control of the humanitarian aid that international groups soon were trucking in along newly bulldozed roads. At a time when fundamentals of life – rice and clean water – were in dire shortage, control of them meant power. Sometimes summary executions of rival fighters was part of the game of securing it.

One day, with a news article to report, I drove a car down 007's new access road. Looking ahead, I saw that the usual teeming entrance area was empty save for a squad of armed men sweeping

Land Bridge feeding station at Nong Chan. Courtesy of Timothy Carney.

past empty huts. I turned the car quickly around and sped back to a permanent road a kilometre out. There I pulled over. Before long came the din of rifles and grenades. It went on for maybe half an hour. A Thai army foot patrol came by, watching, listening, doing nothing to intervene. Soon civilians were streaming out of the forest onto the road, carrying everything they could. It was the same sad scene of flight that Cambodians had endured for the past twenty years. Beyond the fact that this was another Khmer-on-Khmer skirmish, I never found out what exactly happened inside the camp that day.

The Khmer Rouge, operating from other border camps with Thai and Chinese aid, remained united and highly disciplined, inflicting serious casualties on the Vietnamese. Foreign governments wondered, why can't the non-communists do the same? Pressure arose to make them all line up behind one group, the Khmer People's National Liberation Front, headed by Son Sann, an internationally respected man who had been prime minister under Sihanouk in the 1960s. Weapons, food and support in diplomatic forums began flowing to his group. In 007, In Sakhan and his group began to come under armed pressure from Son Sann's militias to join or face consequences. In late 1980, In Sakhan and his men pulled out of the camp after a particularly strong attack and headed for another area of the border.

Later that year Son Sann visited the newly loyal camp with a group of senior aides. As dusk neared, there was a final stop for the group: the Temple of the Black Buddha. The leader stepped down from a van near the west side, then camp officials led him around to the east side. There, like countless Cambodians before him, he burned incense and said prayers before the Black Buddha. With that, the KPNLF put its stamp of control on camp and temple.

Gaffar Peang-Meth, a member of the front's executive council, stayed by the van that afternoon and tried to engage camp officials about political things – the loyalties of the refugees, the nearness of the Vietnamese. But these men wanted only to talk about the temple and its great resident spirit, who by their account was watching at that very moment. People who came with good intentions would be welcomed, they explained. Gaffar was a Muslim, a member of Cambodia's Cham minority, and he had been raised not to believe in such things. But he found himself wondering about this spirit. Had he somehow offended it by coming here? Stepping on fallen stones as he moved around the central courtyard, he began wondering if his feet were offending the spirit. With dark closing in, the thought occurred to him that the spirit might prevent the van from leaving.

It did not; Son Sann returned after about twenty minutes, his party piled in and the van rolled out of the area.

As was clear from what Gaffar saw, many refugees were putting aside the uncertain feelings about the temple that had prevailed in the camp's early days. Sdok Kok Thom was becoming a focus of camp religious life. By 1984, Cambodian monks and nuns had taken up residence in and around the temple. The nuns had huts inside the walls. With UN help, a small cinderblock monastery had been built just beyond the southwest corner of the temple's outer walls for monks. On certain days, monks might be seen relaxing atop the stones of the south library, or nuns meditating in the ruins. Women wearing the white garments of Brahminist spiritual purity processed around walls in hopes of bringing on luck and protection.

The temple was a standard stop for resistance fighters headed for the battlefield. Monks would consecrate holy water, then administer blessings. It was believed that if men went into combat with pure, cleansed hearts, bullets would pass right through their bodies doing no harm. Other people came for blessings for more mundane concerns. And not only from the local camp. By now the temple was drawing people from other camps scattered up and down the border.

Refugees inside Sdok Kok Thom, circa 1979. Courtesy of Roland Neveu.

At times, the central courtyard took on the atmosphere of a village festival. People laid out amulets and other religious items for sale amidst fallen stones. Bread baked in ovens at the camp was put on offer. It was particularly busy on special holidays – Buddhist lent, for instance. Formal services would be held at the cinderblock monastery and afterward people would come to light incense before the Black Buddha.

Sokry Sum, a young man in the camp from its early days, recalls going there many times for the tranquillity, the feeling of peace and spiritual presence. Refugees were in essence prisoners. They couldn't go into Cambodia due to the war there. They couldn't go into Thailand because they were foreigners penned in by Thai police and soldiers. They had to make do where they were. The temple was 'one of the few places where we could go to see something beautiful,' he recalled.

Year after year, the temple kept up its reputation as a zone of the supernatural. One day, people noticed some stone *naga* heads lying where they weren't remembered to have been. Hundreds of

Refugees receive blessing at Sdok Kok Thom, with a member of the Khmer militia visible in the background, 1984. Courtesy of Cameron Macauley.

people came to pray at them, leaving flowers and a veritable forest of incense sticks. Word spread that the images had dug themselves up, though other stories had it that a monk dreamed a dream telling him where to dig.

There were cursory attempts at physical restoration. A tin-roofed shelter was placed over the holy image of Luang Poh Boon Tham. Someone built a door to the chamber of the central sanctuary. The densest of the vegetation in the central courtyard was cleared away, making it possible to cross it without constantly bending and ducking. Some of the soil that had built up over the years, raising the ground level, was removed.

But in the same paradoxical approach shown by Thai villagers a generation earlier, there was also dangerous behaviour. Resistance fighters sometimes loosed bullets in the temple's vicinity. Landmines were seeded on nearby trails. Mine-detecting equipment that resistance fighters had been given to enhance their military muscle was turned to the old task of hunting for gleaming buried treasure. (Like with the Thai villagers, the results seem to have been only disappointment.) But some people appear to have found more of the temple's proven treasure, carved stone, and taken it off for clandestine sale.

Medieval Romans treated the Colosseum as a stone quarry. At Sdok Kok Thom, some resistance fighters did the same, hauling away ancient laterite blocks to use as building material for at least one bunker. Other stones became barriers on an approach road and seats in a makeshift outdoor movie theatre that operated for a time near the temple. And the religious faithful did some damage, using hammers to break off chunks of stone for carving into Buddha images. Monks directed which stones should be mined this way; the provenance of the material would ensure that the resulting images were invested with special holiness.

There was one part of Sadashiva's creation that was put to use in a non-harmful way, the holy reservoir. Its floor was lower than surrounding land, so when well-drilling equipment was brought in to hunt for water during the the dry season, the *baray* was the logical place to begin. Dozens of holes were punched into the reservoir's floor. Some yielded water, some did not. But in the rainy season, the old priest's dikes always captured water falling from the heavens and held it for use by the area's many new residents.

Demining worker uses a metal detector to hunt for left-over munitions at Sdok Kok Thom. Courtesy of General Chatichai Choonhavan Foundation.

Chapter XVII – Lethal Souvenirs

Countless prayers for victory were said at the temple, but subsequent years did not go well for Cambodia's non-communist resistance on the battlefield. In 1984, Vietnamese troops swept up and down the border, destroying camp after camp, including the one around the temple. Son Sann's united resistance army never succeeded in drawing enough blood from the enemy to win.

But prayers for peace were eventually answered. The Cambodian conflict slowly burned itself out. With the power of Hanoi's Soviet patrons crumbling, the last Vietnamese troops went home in 1989. The warring Cambodian factions negotiated a ceasefire. More than 20,000 UN peacekeeping troops and civilian advisers entered the country to oversee an election in 1993. The vote was a long way from clean and peaceful and more turmoil would follow. Still, after a quarter century, Cambodia was no longer at war with itself.

Sdok Kok Thom was back at peace as well. But combatants had left behind a collection of lethal mementos. Some were landmines deliberately planted. Others were excess munitions that had simply been cast aside, as soldiers are wont to do, and were now hidden by foliage. Every so often, a farmer or a water buffalo stepped in the wrong place. Wheelchairs and legless victims became common sights in Thai border communities.

In 1989, Nipon Prompilai was a young boy growing up in the village of Nong Samet. One day, he was walking in the forest with his grandmother. Like any child of his age, he had an eye for shiny things. On this day he spotted something small, plastic on the top, metal on the bottom. For some reason, he beat at it with a stick. It exploded. He survived with limbs intact but spent two months recovering.

But away from the borders, Thailand was experiencing boom times in the '80s. Its exports were selling well in global markets. Standards of living were on the way up, as were government tax revenues and budgets. The Thai Fine Arts Department, custodian of the country's antiquity sites, was moving ahead with a costly program to restore more of the Khmer Empire-era temples that stood on Thai soil. In part the goal was to spur economic development by creating destinations for tourists. Sakaew province, where Sdok Kok Thom stood, could certainly use such a boost, officials knew. But visitors could not be invited to a place where they might trample on explosives. Discussions began as to how to get rid of the things.

Eventually, three groups came together for the job: the Japan Alliance for Humanitarian Demining Support, a private group based in Japan; the General Chatichai Choonhavan Foundation, the charity of a former Thai military officer and prime minister; and the Thailand Mine Action Centre, a Thai government agency coordinating various departments' anti-mine efforts. No one seems to have planned it, but this collaboration was to have a larger effect of giving the temple yet another new identity in its long history: showcase in the anti-landmine movement that was picking up momentum around the world.

In 1997, the American activist Jody Williams and the non-profit group she headed, the International Campaign to Ban Landmines, had won the Nobel Peace Prize. That same year, one hundred twenty-two governments signed a treaty swearing off use of landmines and pledging to clean up lingering minefields within their borders. Sdok Kok Thom and countless other former battlefields in the world were demonstrating day after day that mines remained a cruel threat to local people and livestock decades after the soldiers who laid them had moved on.

For hands-on expertise, the Sdok Kok Thom program turned to a South African named Johan Van Zyl. A former police and military officer, he was part of a cadre of people worldwide who had trained in the military application of explosives and turned their skills later in life to disposing of them. He had experience clearing minefields in conflict zones as far afield as Bosnia, Sri Lanka and Mozambique. Now he took up residence in a hotel in Aranyaprathet and began the new job.

Mine-clearing is dangerous but also tedious work. Land that has become overgrown is often first prepped metre by metre by special armoured tractors that cut away foliage to expose the soil. Then specially trained deminers go over it centimetre by centimetre with dogs or electronic detectors, often on hands and knees.

One of Van Zyl's first tasks was to calm concerns among the program's corporate sponsors in Japan, who loved the goal of clearing mines but were unnerved by the possibility of workers getting hurt. One question they worried over was whether the soil around Sdok Kok Thom hid anti-tank mines, which are much larger and more destructive than the more common varieties that are designed only to kill or maim human beings. Certainly, the Thai army had worried during the conflict that Vietnamese tanks would come crashing across the border here. If such mines were out there, an anti-tank tractor might accidentally detonate one and kill the vehicle's operator. But Van Zyl, who knew his minefields and battlefield tactics, had tramped all around the area, sizing it up, and concluded that it was highly unlikely that there were anti-tank mines here. He flew to Japan to talk to the donors. They were not easily convinced: how can you know what's underground? they asked. Eventually, they put their trust in his judgement.

Work got underway. On charts, the clearance zone was divided into blocks, some of them small so that workers could quickly finish them and feel a sense of progress in the long job. There was a special deadline for one of the zones, the *baray*. Work had to be completed there before the start of the wet season, when Sadashiva's earthworks would capture and retain rain water.

Each day, Van Zyl rode out in a car from Aranyaprathet, while another vehicle picked up local men, most of them farmers who had been recruited and trained as deminers. The job of clearing vegetation with the tractors went fairly smoothly. Van Zyl's call had been correct – the vehicles set off no anti-tank mines.

With the ground exposed, the work got down-and-dirty. Each deminer, wearing body armour, helmets and visors for protection, moved slowly along a designated strip of land, passing the sensor of an Italian-made metal detector back and forth over the soil. In

Demining worker removes a rocket grenade. at Sdok Kok Thom.
Courtesy of General Chatichai Choonhavan Foundation.

some cases, a dog that had been trained to sniff for explosives acted as the detector, working on a leash with a handler. If the animal signalled it had smelled something, a second dog was brought in to confirm it.

Any positive signal led the deminer to stop, mark the spot with a small flag, then get down on hands and knees for the very delicate job of probing the object from the side, with a knife. Often these were Soviet-design bayonets that Van Zyl had picked up in border markets. Soil was meticulously removed from around the object. In almost every case, it turned out to be harmless metal. There was a danger of people growing careless in a job that rarely found anything dangerous. So to keep spirits up and concentration focused, Van Zyl pledged and paid a small cash prize from his own pocket to the first man who found an actual piece of explosives.

One by one, other pieces of munitions were uncovered and destroyed in controlled explosions. Six months into the job came other confirmation that the job had a real purpose: an officer of the Thai Border Patrol Police stepped on a mine about three hundred metres from the clearing zone. One man in the patrol lost a leg at the knee; another was slightly injured. The demining team expanded its work to include the area where the mine went off.

As the work progressed, Van Zyl became sort of a tour guide, showing friends and visitors not only the mine-clearing work but the temple, which kindled in him the same kind of fascination I had felt those years earlier. In a more formal way, the Thai government put the temple on display to international demining officials. In September 2003, Bangkok hosted a working meeting of parties to the landmine ban treaty, known as the Ottawa Convention. On a break from lengthy conference sessions, about three hundred delegates from all over the world put on casual clothes and flew up from Bangkok. Demining workers ran through their paces as cameras clicked. When a shopping centre opens, honoured guests snip ribbons; when a ship is launched they crack champagne bottles against the hull. Here the equivalent flourish of ceremony was carried out by Thailand's ambassador to the United Nations in Geneva, Laxanachantorn Laohaphan. She pressed a button and some of the recovered explosives went boom, destroyed forever.

After thirteen months, the program wrapped up with 410,000 square metres of land cleared at a cost of $1.4 million. The team located a total of 220,000 pieces of metal scrap. Of those, just seventy-eight were deadly explosives, enough to kill plenty of people, surely, but also a demonstration of the high cost of neutralising a hazard that soldiers can create in an hour or two. The operation ended with the most important statistic in mine clearing: zero casualties among the deminers.

To show the travelling public just how friendly a place Sdok Kok Thom had become, Thai officials brought contestants in a Thai beauty pageant to the temple, where they posed for photos at the eastern gate. A final ceremony in 2004 declared the temple safe and secure.

Sdok Kok Thom continues to function as a showcase for demining experts. In the spring of 2009, Bangkok hosted another meeting of parties to the anti-landmine treaty and organised another trip to the border. At Sdok Kok Thom, dancers entertained them. Thailand is under international pressure to meet treaty-stipulated deadlines for clearing its mines and places like Sdok Kok Thom are offered up as evidence that officials are committed and work is proceeding apace. Developing countries are often on the look-out for aid funds for the costly task. If mine-clearing can open the way to tourism, as it did at the temple, governments can often tap economic development funds in addition to ones set aside for humanitarian projects.

Van Zyl says that as landmines go, the ones his teams found around the temple were relatively easy to clear. There were no organised fields, there were none of the advanced, hard-to-detect plastic models and none of the notoriously hard to clear trip-wire designs. The recovered mines were for the most part made in Vietnam or other Soviet-bloc countries. Others appeared to be from China.

Who laid the mines? There is a tendency today to blame every Cambodian problem of the last four decades on the Khmer Rouge. But they do not appear to have ever controlled the temple site. On the other hand, Van Zyl cautions against concluding that the Soviet-bloc origin of most of the recovered mines means that the pro-Soviet Vietnamese and their Cambodian allies were mainly to blame. In conflict zones there is often a back-door trade in munitions even between the opposing sides. And the anti-communist resistance fighters were usually armed with Soviet-bloc weapons, obtained no one would quite say where. Another possible explanation is the Thai army, which certainly had mines in its arsenals during the conflict. From 1975 to 1979, it was concerned with keeping out Khmer Rouge raiding parties. After 1979, it was concerned with keeping out the Vietnamese.

Whoever laid them, the weapons are gone. The temple that Sadashiva built and the lands he owned around it are again safe.

Old sandstone placed atop new laterite wall, Sdok Kok Thom, 2009.

Chapter XVIII – Restoration

Applying backhoes and power tools to historic monuments always raises ethical, even metaphysical questions. Should the goal be only to shore up what the ages have given us and prevent further damage? Or should it be to make the building what it was on the day it was completed? And is there any legitimate value in the romantic stirrings that ruins cause in so many hearts? Meeting in 1964 in Venice, the second International Congress of Architects and Technicians of Historic Monuments agreed on theoretically universal principles of restoration. Among them: thorough archaeological and historical study must precede any restoration; modern technology may be used if the traditional methods proved inadequate; no additions should be made to the building; replacement components should be clearly distinguishable from originals. Today countries generally praise the so-called Venice Charter yet in practice apply a potpourri of interpretations derived from issues of budget, depth of understanding of a building's original appearance, local sensibilities and the expectations of tourists.

For instance, historians have long believed that the Parthenon in Athens was in its day painted in bright colours. Yet the modern eye associates Greek antiquity with the monochrome of bare stone and that is what the classic building today shows its visitors and likely always will – even if by some miracle we came to know its precise colours of 2,500 years ago.

Dresden's Church of Our Lady, the Frauenkirche, casualty of the allied firebombing of 1945, has risen anew after lying as a pile of scorched rubble for half a century. The restorers' objective was to bring back the church as it had existed on its completion date in 1743. Yet what stands today is in a fundamental way different – most of its stones are replacements, the new ones showing light-hued against the dark colour of the weathered old ones.

The colonial French were the first to grapple with questions of reconstruction concerning the Khmer monuments. Some they rebuilt meticulously, others they left largely as found. At the Ta Prohm temple, for instance, they kept in place the mammoth fig and silk-cotton trees that had been growing for decades if not centuries from cracks in the ancient stones. That sight is today one of Angkor's most popular and the cause of endless photos and descriptive excess in postcards and emails home.

In 1992, the UN Educational, Scientific and Cultural Organisation declared the Angkor region a World Heritage Site. Since then, foreign money has poured in for restoration. Individual governments and private organisations have adopted individual structures. The Chinese have rebuilt the temple Chau Sey Tevoda, the Japanese have refurbished a library at the Bayon, the Italians have stabilised a brick tower at Pre Rup, to name just a few of the projects. Each national team brings to its site some of its home-grown approach – and there has been spirited disagreement as to whose is best.

Thailand has experienced little debate like this, beyond the occasional newspaper column and Internet posting. The Fine Arts Department, which oversees the country's Khmer-era monuments, in general calls the shots and has opted for strong, assertive intervention. The largest of the Khmer temples in the country, Phimai, was painstakingly put back together starting in the 1960s using an approach known in the trade as anastylosis, reconstruction using recovered fallen parts, with substitutes for ones that are missing. Phnom Rung, another Khmer temple in Thailand, got a similar make-over, rendering it so perfect that you might wonder at the gate if you've stepped through a time warp.

Critics of anastylosis contend that this type of restoration in effect eradicates history. In their view, the ruined state of a monument is part of its inviolable identity. And since original building plans don't exist, they say, anastylosis risks putting things back together in a way they never were. Thai Fine Arts officials have heard these arguments and remain deeply committed to the approach. They say that today's visitors should get the same architectural experience that those of ancient times did and that the precise original appearance can be determined through meticulous surveys and research. Some officials go on to dismiss love of ruins as sentimentality. To me there may be also an element of a deeply held Thai belief that the most holy temple, the one through which the most merit for the next life will be earned, is a new one. As for the ancient ones, they can at least be made to look new.

In the 1990s, even before the land mines were cleared, the Fine Arts Department took on Sdok Kok Thom's outer east gate. Recovered stones that had survived in good condition were returned to their determined former places. Concrete substitutes were made for damaged or missing ones, then painted to look like stone.

Following a lengthy Brahmin ceremony meant to propitiate the temple's spirit, work began on the inner courtyard area after 2000. Crews uprooted trees and pulled out vines. The ground that I'd walked in 1979 was a good metre or so higher than its level in Sadashiva's time. So shovel teams dug it down to the original level, bringing back into view the massive laterite bases on which the

Irregular shapes of sandstone blocks at Sdok Kok Thom has helped in the job of putting stones in their original places.

sandstone structures stood.

A new restoration philosophy was to govern the program now: all visible replacement components would be made from the same materials with which the original Khmer builders had worked, sandstone and laterite. Concrete would be used only for components that didn't show.

Restorers completely disassembled sections of the temple that had survived in relatively good shape. That was done in part to address the chronic weak foundations of Khmer buildings. The courtyard's galleries, for instance, were in places underpinned originally by just a thin layer of laterite. The stonework above had weighed heavily over the centuries, breaking that layer. So, after disassembling the galleries, reconstruction workers dug deep foundation trenches. They poured concrete at the bottom, then placed multiple layers of laterite on top of that. All of this would be hidden, so use of concrete was deemed acceptable. The original stonework, together with substitute blocks where needed, was reassembled on top. Now it stood on foundations that would last indefinitely.

The more challenging job was the temple's collapsed sections. One by one, fallen stones were gathered, catalogued, numbered and laid out in collection areas on ground outside the temple. The work was slow, by modern standards, at least. Most of the stones were so big they had to be moved by crane, one by one. Once a year, worked stopped for another Brahmin ceremony to win the spirit's acceptance.

In the reconstruction of the Frauenkirche in Dresden, architects worked with the aid of the architect's original plans and with computers that digitally compared the shapes of recovered stones and suggested which might fit where. At Sdok Kok Thom, there was no such help. Workers and supervisors relied on lessons they had learned at previous rebuildings of Khmer monuments in Thailand. Architect Vasu Poshyanandana, who oversees the project, says the job proceeded generally smoothly. Key members of the team had gained an innate appreciation of the intentions, plans and techniques of the long-ago builders. The job progressed with Vasu giving guidance on how stylistic trends in the temple's period would have affected stones' placement.

If a particular fallen block had been carved with sculpture, the man-made lines and forms gave important clues as to how it fitted together with its neighbours. Also helpful was that Sadashiva's masons, following an approach common in those days, seem not to have cared whether stones were symmetrical, as long as they fit snugly together into a pleasing whole. Restorers examining a collapsed well would often find that its blocks had unique, oddball forms that could go back together in only one way, like jigsaw puzzle pieces of random shapes. Moving the stones around in trial-and-error experimentation could eventually reveal the original combination.

One of the toughest jobs was the central sanctuary, laid low in the 1960s by the villagers' explosives. Many of the stones had been broken, others had been carried off, others had eroded. Vasu and the team spent long months analysing the stones recovered from the courtyard. He concluded that the sanctuary had had four tiers, topped with a classic Khmer element, a large stone lotus blossom. 'I am sure of the original form,' he explained to me. 'We have information from every level, every layer of stone.'

Central sanctuary, Sdok Kok Thom, 2009.

A mason shaping a sandstone replacement block, Sdok Kok Thom, 2009.

Those few parts of the sanctuary that were still standing were taken apart. The structure's foundations were strengthened with concrete, ancient blocks of laterite and quite a few new ones. Then rebuilding began. Over many months, the tower rose again, encased in scaffolding, old stones coming together with new. Sandstone taken straight from the ground (its source was a quarry in Northeastern Thailand) has a clean white hue. So there was no mistaking the new stones. Missing *naga* heads were carved as simple shapes, without details, so that there would be no question that they were replacements.

Today the tower extends above the forest canopy, visible from far away. It and everything below it, says Vasu, were restored following the principles of the Venice Charter.

Work continued. In early 2010, workers were using picks and crowbars to dismantle collapsed sections of the outer laterite wall. With the help of a backhoe, stones were moved one at a time a few metres away to await reconstruction, each one bearing a number that indicated where the ancient masons had placed it. The plan calls for laying concrete foundations, then putting the walls back up as they once were, this time more able to withstand the ages. Sections of wall that had made it through to modern times in good shape were meanwhile being reinforced in place. As this task progressed, work was underway to restore the pediments of the 'libraries', to dig out the moats between inner and outer wall and refill them with water. One day I watched a diesel excavator do battle with a tree stump at an edge of an eastern moat.

Coming up on the work schedule was to remove the visible concrete replacement parts that were put in the reconstructed outer east *gopura* and replace them with ones crafted from original materials.

Vasu expressed hope that at some point in the future a replica of the inscription stone will be placed at the temple. That would make the reconstruction truly complete.

Thai-Cambodian Border Marker 53 during the refugee crisis. Courtesy of Timothy Carney.

Chapter XIX – Holy Ground Contested

Few Cambodians know of Sdok Kok Thom, but those who do will often tell you that the Thais stole it.

The sad fact is that many of the territorial disputes that vexed the Siamese and French authorities a century ago live on today. The successive governments that have ruled Cambodia since its independence in 1953 – royalist, republican, Khmer Rouge, communist, reformed communist – have differed over many things, but not in distrust of the country next door. The same holds true in Bangkok. Despite centuries-old similarities in language, culture and religion, there is little love between the two countries. One of the issues that won't go away is: who owns the ancient Khmer temples that lie along the common border?

On this question the focus is Preah Vihear, possessed of the most astonishing settings of all the temples the ancient Khmers built: the top of a 525-metre cliff. Located in the Dangrek Mountain range, Preah Vihear has a rare linear lay-out and a north-south orientation that is another breaking of the mould. On a visit in 1973, I found that its entrance steps, at its northern end, gave little hint of the amazing things that lay beyond. As I made my way up the gentle incline, I came to a series of ever-more elaborate avenues and sanctuaries. Inscriptions depict Preah Vihear as a place of miracles, where gods come to earth. Standing at the cliff top, gazing down on a forested plain, I had no trouble understanding how the ancients deemed this holy ground.

For centuries, there was no question about ownership. Preah Vihear was built by the Khmers, on land deep inside their empire. But at some point the temple passed into the hands of the ascendant Siam, which in the 18th century formally annexed entire provinces of Cambodia. Early in the 20th century, the French compelled Siam to return annexed lands, including Angkor. There remained now the task of deciding exactly where the new border would run. A Siamese-French commission began work on that question, with a common understanding that in the north the border would be the watershed line of the Dangrek Mountain Range, which runs roughly east-west. This basically meant that places where rain water flowed north toward the Khorat Plateau would be Siamese, and where it flowed south would be Cambodian. A joint Siamese-French team travelled the range in 1907 to conduct reconnaissance. Among the stops was Preah Vihear temple, situated in the Dangrek range.

The Siamese were not up on the latest techniques of cartography, so when it came time to actually draw up a map of the border, the task went to the French. In the autumn of 1907, they produced a map that showed the border following the east-west peak ridges of the Dangreks and making a loop north around Preah Vihear temple. The temple was shown as being in Cambodia.

In 1908, the map was formally sent to the Siamese government. Its officials must have noticed whose soil the temple was shown on. But they seem not to have cared. The unusual topography of the site gave Siam practical control – reaching the temple from the Siamese north was a simple stroll up a gently sloping hill. From the Cambodian south, it demanded rock-climbing skills, a conquest of that sheer cliff.

In 1953 the French headed home and Prince Sihanouk became head of a newly sovereign Cambodia. Soon his government was complaining that Thai forces were illegally occupying Preah Vihear. In 1959, the Cambodians filed suit at the World Court in the Hague seeking a decision affirming that the temple was theirs. The case drew wide international attention, in part due to the spectacular nature of the thing in contest. The Cambodians retained former U.S. secretary of state Dean Acheson to argue their case. A former British attorney general, Frank Soskice, signed on to represent the Thais. Former Thai prime minister Seni Pramoj, a British-trained lawyer, was also on the Thai team.

Lawyers are paid to muster whatever arguments they can. So much of the proceedings in the Peace Palace, as the court's neo-Renaissance building in the Hague is known, had nothing directly to do with the temple. Thailand, for instance, pursued a lengthy challenge of the court's jurisdiction, contending that a ruling in a case in which Israel had sued Bulgaria proved its point. Over the course of arguments on this issue, the court heard lengthy expositions concerning the meaning of the English word 'renew.' Cambodia claimed that in a 1950 declaration to the United Nations,

Discarded field artillery still visible at Preah Vihear as of early 2008. Courtesy of Stephen A. Murphy.

View from the base of the stairway leading to Preah Vihear.
Courtesy of Stephen A. Murphy.

Thailand had used the word in a way that implied that it accepted the court's jurisdiction. Thailand said that in fact the word had been misused in that declaration – Thailand had therefore not accepted jurisdiction. Cambodian counsel Acheson fired back with a learned speech in which he quoted uses of the word by St. Paul, Horace and Shakespeare to argue that the Thais knew exactly what it meant and therefore had accepted jurisdiction. The court ruled against the Thais on this issue.

When it came time to consider the real issue, ownership, the court did not much concern itself with claims by Cambodians that they were the temple's rightful owner, because their country was heir to the glories of Angkor. Nor did it listen much to Thai declarations of a nation's right to defend sacred soil. 'Since our nation became established in the present peninsula six hundred years ago,' Seni had told the court, 'our frontiers have fluctuated with our fortunes. But never have we been forced beyond the ramparts of the Dangrek range of mountains.' The Thai public, he said, was deeply concerned that the Cambodians were seeking 'a foothold on territory which has always been Thai.'

Rather, what mattered most to the court was that 1907 map and the two sides' official dealings or lack of dealings concerning it in subsequent years.

As the case proceeded in the Palace of Justice, the team representing Cambodia argued that the map was a binding document. It clearly showed Preah Vihear on their side of the line. The Thais' lawyers argued that the map was wrong. Before

Thai soldiers patrol near a Thai-Cambodia border marker during the refugee crisis. Courtesy of Timothy Carney.

it was drawn up, they pointed out, both sides had agreed that the mountains' watershed line would be the border. Preah Vihear, which extends north from the edge of the great cliff, was clearly in the range's Thai watershed, the Thais said. Therefore the temple was theirs.

On 15 June 1962, the court finally spoke. It acknowledged that the two sides had agreed to make the watershed line the border. But the court declined to rule on where the watershed line ran. That was not the issue, in the court's view. The issue was how the Siamese and then Thais had behaved toward the map in the half a century since its creation. In subsequent border talks with the French, the court said, they had never objected to the map's depiction of Preah Vihear's location. Moreover, certain maps published in Siam showed the temple as being in Cambodia. In 1930, Prince Damrong himself had been received at the temple by a French colonial official, which to the court seemed a Siamese acknowledgment of French and Cambodian sovereignty. These long years of silence, the court ruled, amounted to acceptance under international law. The Thais had been happy to benefit from other provisions of the border treaty, the ruling noted, but now they were demanding the abrogation of a section that they belatedly found objectionable. The court rejected Thai arguments that their side had not understood the map or felt no need to object because it had practical control of the temple.

Case closed: Preah Vihear belongs to Cambodia.

Thai protesters quickly thronged the streets of Bangkok; their leaders announced they would boycott a meeting of the Southeast Asia Treaty Organisation, the West's main military alliance at that time. Much anger was directed at Washington – to many Thais, Dean Acheson's service on Cambodia's legal team meant that Washington had taken sides.

Eventually cooler heads prevailed in Bangkok. The government formally accepted the ruling. In January 1963, Prince Sihanouk himself made the arduous climb up the cliff to personally take control of the temple at a ceremony attended by close to a thousand people.

Half a century later, the World Court affair continues to rankle Thais. And at the same time, Cambodians can respond with anger when Thais even suggest they have rights to the Angkorian heritage.

In 2003, Thai media reports quoting a Thai soap opera actress as saying that Angkor belonged to her country led mobs of Cambodians to attack the Thai embassy in Phnom Penh, setting it afire. Thai-owned businesses in the city got the same treatment. With the Cambodian police largely standing aside, the Thai air force sent transport planes to Phnom Penh to evacuate Thai citizens. By the time the violence subsided, almost $50 million in damage had been done, the Thai government estimated.

In 2008, tensions over Preah Vihear came back to a boil after Cambodia applied to UNESCO to designate the temple as a World Heritage Site.

Though the Thais surrendered the temple following the World Court decision, they had remained in control of small parcels of adjacent land that the 1907 map also showed as being in Cambodia. Cambodia's application to UNESCO, some Thais complained, included some of that adjacent land and thus was an effort to take it over. Protesters marched on the temple and tried to plant the Thai flag. The Cambodians closed off access from Thailand. Troops from both countries' armies moved into the area. They took up positions within metres of each other, settling in for a long stay. They traded fire more than once, killing a number of soldiers. Partisans meanwhile took the fight to the Internet, exchanging insults in blogs and wrestling for control of the temple's article in the online Wikipedia encyclopaedia. Insults and arguments inserted into the article were so strong that Wikipedia administrators froze access to it. Meanwhile, UNESCO approved the Cambodian application.

And what of Sdok Kok Thom, another border temple? In 2003, the year of the blow-up over Angkor, Bangkok newspapers reported that the government in Phnom Penh had sent a letter to the Thai Ministry of Foreign Affairs claiming sovereignty over Sdok Kok Thom. A spate of protest marches followed in Sakaew province, with local Thais expressing anger over the idea of losing one of their province's greatest prides, not to mention a source of growing tourist revenue. The issue died down of its own accord, but some Thai commentators predicted it would return. By one theory, part of the Cambodians' motivation was a belief that getting Sdok Kok Thom would also move the demarcation line in the Gulf of Thailand, giving Cambodia a bigger share of oil reserves there.

Cambodia did not pursue its claim, nor did it give it up. In early 2010, a newsletter published by the Cambodian embassy in Paris publicly stated it again: Sdok Kok Thom was in Cambodian territory, an article in the newsletter declared, offering no elaboration, but had come under Thai control in 2002. 'To go to the site of this edifice dating to the XIth Century, the Cambodian visitor must therefore cross the border and request specific permission from Thai guards,' the article complained. Thais had taken over Cambodian rice fields in the area as well, it said.

There is no chain-link fence, no stream or river marking exactly where the two countries come together near Sdok Kok Thom. Rather the border is a collection of imaginary lines running between numbered stone markers that the French and Siamese put in place early in the 20th century. Thais say that those stones' locations show clearly that the border runs east of the temple, placing it in Thailand; Cambodians contend that Thais have moved some of the stones in recent times.

If the issue ever goes to court, lawyers for the Thai side will no doubt point to French statements of the early 20th century that the 1907 demarcation placed the temple just inside Siamese territory. Aymonier fulminated about that. The Sanskrit linguist Louis Finot simply stated it as fact. 'The new frontier passes just to the east of Sdok Kok Thom, which has remained in Siam,' he wrote in a 1915 journal article. Also bolstering Thai arguments would be modern maps that show the temple in Thailand and the fact that Thais official and unofficial appear to have had practical control of the site since the demarcation, with the exception of the refugee period. It was a Thai District Officer who came to investigate Monk Long Nails' alleged treasure-hunting around 1920, not a French or Cambodian. It is Thai writing that labels the image of Luang Poh Boon Tham and it was Thai villagers who carried off the temple's sculpted stone for sale to art dealers. And it is Thai authorities who today administer the temple, have built a road to it and financed its reconstruction.

But points like these would put hardly a dent in the convictions of Cambodians that Sdok Kok Thom can only belong to the people whose forebears built it. And the war experience reinforced feelings of ownership. Refugees arriving at Camp 007, with its many thousands of Cambodians and hardly a Thai in sight, could not be faulted for concluding they were on their own country's soil. The

Nationalistic sentiments abound at Preah Vihear as can be seen in this sign placed near the temple's entrance in early 2008. Courtesy of Stephen A. Murphy.

presence of a stunning monument of the Khmer heritage seemed to be further confirmation of that. When the Thai army built a kilometres-long ditch and berm defensive line passing several hundred metres west of the temple, many refugees concluded that this line must mark the border – where else would the Thais put such a fortification, intended to stop any advancing Vietnamese tanks? And when the refugees finally left the temple site, Thai forces moved in to secure it. To Cambodians, that seemed like a seizure of territory.

If those court proceedings ever take place, legal counsel for the Cambodians will no doubt cite those events and also point to statements that high-ranking Thais made during the refugee crisis. At the time, Thailand was shoring up Khmer Rouge and anti-communist resistance forces against the Vietnamese even as it was publicly claiming neutrality in the conflict. We do not tolerate the presence of armed guerrillas on our soil, Thai officials declared – we disarm any fighters who cross into Thailand. By the logic of these statements, camps such as 007 where resistance fighters walked around with AK-47s and rocket grenades had to be in Cambodian territory. Leaders of the resistance voiced the same claim, which for them had the political advantage of making their stronghold a liberated zone rather than a foreign sanctuary. Some senior U.S. diplomats accepted the claim, staying out of 007 on grounds that going in would mean entering foreign territory. Many journalists at the time took this all to be diplomatic expedience meant to mask Thailand's support of the anti-Vietnamese forces during the war.

Sadly, no Thai-Cambodian consensus is in sight concerning Sdok Kok Thom.

'To say it belongs to Thailand is a lie and Thailand has no shame at all,' a Cambodia partisan wrote on a blog in 2008. Someone from the other point of view had this to offer: 'Idiot Khmers here. This temple is IN Thailand boundary.'

Visiting school children leaving through the outer eastern *gopura*, Sdok Kok Thom, 2009.

Chapter XX – The Temple Today

Thirty years it has been. I am sitting in the cab of a pick-up truck, riding through rice fields that are brown and stubbly, awaiting the next cycle of rains. And ahead – something strange, half hidden in the foliage. I get that long-ago quickened heart beat.

The idea for this book had come to me in 2006 and since then, I had been running down old photos, making my way through the prose of Aymonier and Coedès. I'd been looking at Thai blogs about the temple, trading emails with people in various countries who might have something of interest. Each new fact gathered brought a feeling of celebration.

In October 2008 I took an early retirement from my long-time employer, *The Washington Post*. Now was my chance.

In January I flew to Bangkok, where for two weeks I did interviews about the temple and trolled libraries and museums. On the streets of the city I'd known so many years before, I felt like a rube. Bangkok now had the elevated Skytrain transit system, fashion shoots atop glass high-rises and VIP movie tickets at twenty bucks apiece. But, having read up on the Hindu tradition, I had new awareness of how the old ways hung on in the city. On a sidewalk I came across a gold-painted Brahma shrine one night, the four-faced god illuminated by an electric bulb and tended by tiny elephant images. I looked down from a Skytrain car one day on a giant *garuda* bird god that is the symbol of the huge Bangkok Bank.

I took a bus to Aranyaprathet, the nearest Thai town of any size to Sdok Kok Thom. Aranyaprathet was quite different too. A lot larger, with Internet cafes, ATMs and at least one very modern and efficient optician shop – I stopped in to replace a pair of glasses I had left in a Bangkok taxi. The next morning I got up early and went to the bus station to buy a ticket to the temple, about thirty kilometres away. Sorry, I was told. No bus goes there. In my day, you could wait by any rural Thai road and sooner or later some kind of public transport would come along – a bus, a truck with benches in the back, a shared taxi. But the country people of Thailand had come up in the world in my absence. They now had wheels of their own. So, I struck a deal with a genial pick-up driver named Vichien Charernporn for private transport. Off we went, toward what was sure to be the biggest time-lapse shock of all.

We headed north up a highway, then turned east onto smaller roads that passed through rice fields. They were quiet, peaceful now, as if dusty from dry season privation. There was no sign of the Royal Thai Army. No roadblocks. Every few kilometres, a large blue sign announced reassuringly that Sdok Kok Thom was not far ahead.

Then there it is, its stones showing through the leaves of a grove.

I am one of those sentimental lovers of ruins. And these particular ruins I'd felt I *owned*. Having seen photos on the Internet of what was going on here, I am now prepared for disillusionment, or some kind of unjustified resentment that I've been robbed of my rights. Or just an urge to turn up my nose at architectural bad taste. But when I get out of the truck, none of those feelings arises. It comes to me that this is a remarkable site in history that, like Angkor, is being opened to the world.

I take a few steps, breathing in pleasantly cool country air. Now I have a clear view of the sanctuary. Its new appearance requires some getting used to, yes. I take a minute. Yet...I like it. Stones are back where Sadashiva intended them. Other people, I know, would not share my view.

So on that day and subsequent ones, the temple and I get reacquainted. I tramp all around it. I take hundreds of pictures. I chat with people rebuilding it, visiting it, carrying on their chores in the farmland around it. I visit a nearby school. But most of the time I am alone, and the truth is I very much like that and feel a bit put off when people step into my viewfinder and ruin a deserted shot I'm setting up.

But really, I have no right to umbrage.

So now we go on one more tour, the Sdok Kok Thom of the modern age, the one that shows clearly on Google Earth images.

We start just beyond the temple's north outer wall. It's noisy ground now, a mason's workshop. Perhaps there was one right here a thousand years ago. Rough blocks of sandstone, trucked in from a quarry in Nakorn Ratchasima province to the north, are being worked into replacement parts. The tools are both old and new. First a man with an electric saw creates parallel grooves across the face of a stone. Then another man steps in with hammer and chisel and one by one whacks away the stone between those grooves. Chips and dust fly. The stone block emerges from the process a couple of centimetres thinner. These are made-to-order, customised stones. They'll go into the new inner south wall. Looking on is a supervisor, who holds a chart that shows the future location of each of the stones.

Nearby are some ancient *naga* heads, resting on the soil, awaiting eventual installation in the temple's heights. So – not all of them were bundled off in refugee days. Perhaps I am even seeing the one whose fate I wondered about in 1979.

I move to the inner north wall. There, worn laterite blocks have been taken away and replaced with new ones, which have an almost bright orange hue. Atop them, original sandstone cornice sections are being put back in place. One by one the huge stones are attached to a rope sling and lifted by a crane, its engine racing, then lowered. Workers move in with crowbars to lever the old stones snug together.

Visitors at the main sanctuary, Sdok Kok Thom, 2009.

Sometimes the fit's not quite right, so they signal to the crane operator to lift the stone back off. With hammers and chisels, they do a bit more shaping to the new laterite, then try again.

The men, I discover, are Cambodians, not Thais. Perhaps they've been hired for some special affinity with their forebears? No, Cambodians get the work because they accept lower wages than Thais. This is one thing that hasn't changed, the imbalance of wealth between the two countries.

One of the men, Sopha Jit, trades a few words with me between whacks of his hammer. Does he ever think of the people who first built this place? Often, he replies. And what does he think about them? It was easy to build these things in the ancient days, he says. Now it's hard. He's got work to do, so I step away. Certainly he knows first-hand what an exhausting job this is now. But back then? I strikes me that his words are a modern-day version of the explanations that Henri Mouhot heard in the villages near Angkor: the temples built themselves, they were built by gods. How could human beings have done such a thing?

I'm getting hungry. Out in the dusty parking area, a woman at a wooden stall sells sticky rice and grilled chicken, a standard of the northeastern Thai palate. Plus soft drinks and bottled water. They hit the spot. So does the shade. She comes here most every day, she says, bringing along her two and a half year-old grandson. Sdok Kok Thom is her bread and butter, as it is for the masons and a man who comes here with a digital camera and printer in his car.

We hear the deep grumbling of diesel engines. Two Daimler double-decker buses, frosted windows all around, are pulling in. Passengers step down. They're from a school in the far south of Thailand, up here on a tour. Pornprapa Sakulpram, a volunteer guide from a local community, leads them through the gate in the outer west wall, keeping up a steady stream of facts and figures. This is the back door you've just passed through, she says. In ancient days villagers used this entrance to come inside to work. No, she tells one man, there's no danger from bombs here – they've all been cleared away. This is a safety zone.

Thirty minutes later, the group returns to the buses. The man with the camera snapped portraits of some of the visitors as they went in; now he's offering personalised souvenirs – your face in a

A full-scale replica of the inscription stone presides over the library of Tupprayapittaya School in Sakaew province. Students act as volunteer guides at the temple, located about 12 kilometres from the school.

framed picture of the temple. The price is one hundred baht, about three U.S. dollars. A few people take him up on the offer.

Soon the visitors are filing back on board the buses.

The temple is attracting growing numbers of tourists and students, a flow that pleases many people in the surrounding communities, not to mention economic development officials. Still, getting to the temple takes real effort. Many people choose the easier way of experiencing it, at least in replica. They go to the Ancient City, the historical park outside Bangkok, where they can walk around a roughly one-half scale reproduction of the temple's central courtyard and sanctuary.

The guide Pornprapa directs me to the local school from which she had recently graduated. It is a trim and orderly place. English teachers Thanawat Sumrankit and Nipon Prompilai show me around when I visit on a later day. Nipon, it turns out, grew up in Nong Samet village – it was he who was severely wounded by discarded explosives as a boy. Not a few of the students seem quite proud to live so close to something this special; some serve, like Pornprapa, as volunteer tour guides.

In the school's library – a full-scale replica of the inscription stone. It's made of wood, with calligraphy by a Buddhist priest who specialises in old script and faithfully reproduced each character. All in all, it looks quite like the real thing. It owes its existence to a former deputy district officer, Apichat Tawepoka, who campaigned to raise local awareness of the temple and wrote his own book about it.

I give a talk to a class about the temple. It occurs to me that some of the students listening may be direct descendants of Sadashiva.

Back at the temple, I go for a walk in surrounding farmland, much of which became unusable during the refugee crisis. I run into Phoe Ratanasuwan, 69, who's herding some cattle across a dry rice field. Not surprisingly, he knows precisely how many – twenty-six. He's responsible for each one. 'When they're as big as small elephants, each one weighing a thousand kilos, they'll be sent to Vietnam,' he explains. Cattle husbandry is a sign of rising incomes around here. Phoe offers further evidence of that by going on to mention that he's got a sister in Switzerland.

I head in another direction to see if I can find remnants of the old refugee camp. No success at all – there's not one trace I can see to signal that people numbering in the hundreds of thousands were once here. It's a sign of how quickly nature moves to re-assert itself, but also, I think, of how thoroughly the area was cleared up.

The ancient Khmers' creations do not disappear so easily, however. I discover that I'm walking along the spine of a ten-metre wide embankment that extends north from the temple for close to a kilometre. I remember now – I heard about this thing in Bangkok. It was built around the same time as the temple likely as part of a water management scheme.

'The ground is high up here,' observes Samlee Japjon, an elderly gentleman whom I encounter on the levy. He is out hunting birds with a very long-barrelled rifle. 'So the water collects down there and floods the field.'

Now back to the temple. It is late afternoon. Most of the people are gone. I decide to walk its full holy avenue, to imagine I am the priest who created it.

I start at the reservoir, feeling a bit self-conscious. Standing on the east bank, I gaze across the pleasant grass and trees that now make up its floor. I try to imagine the water that once filled it, the swans of Sadashiva's time gliding across its glittering surface. Then I turn and slowly walk the processional avenue toward the outer eastern *gopura*. Hold on, I think to myself, this isn't realistic. If I were the priest, I would be walking barefoot across the rough laterite pavement. But my shoes stay on. And it's a funny thing – I gauge my breathing and find that my mind is not running off in random directions, as often it does.

I pause half way down the avenue and peer through the doors of the *gopura*. The view into holy ground is as before. I continue on to the door. I put hands together in the sign of greeting and respect of this part of the world, then climb the three laterite steps, cross the moonstone, and emerge at the second, inner avenue. Another walk, another two-handed greeting of entry, then I am through the inner *gopura* and looking across the courtyard. How many times did the priest do this? Did he feel, as I do, that the outlines of the stone structures, their trueness to rules of mathematics, their subtle differences in colour of stone, signal divine inspiration?

I process three times around the main sanctuary, a custom that is common in Thailand and Cambodia today. Then I remove my shoes, and climb those very steep eleven steps to the sanctuary. I am barefoot now, and my feet do hurt, but they should, because the climb to heaven does not come without pain. I feel a bit uneasy, as to whether, even in these modern times, I have a right to enter this chamber. I pass inside.

The old priest stood here, in this cramped space. Before him was the *linga*, the embodiment of Shiva. It was impossible to draw nearer to heaven than this.

Standing alone, I strain to sense the presence of divinity.

It doesn't quite come, just as it doesn't when I do the same at my church at home.

My pilgrimage is done. I descend the steps.

But later I reflect that perhaps the fascination that this place has created in me for so many years, indeed as has religious architecture of pretty much any kind – perhaps that engagement is an expression of the presence which would not reveal itself as I stood there silently demanding that it do so.

Morning in the inner courtyard, Sdok Kok Thom, 2009.

An informal shrine at Sdok Kok Thom, 1979.

Chapter XXI – Why Sadashiva Wrote

As of 2009, Sadashiva's successor at Sdok Kok Thom was an aged Buddhist priest bearing the holy name Luang Poh Suwan Kanthathamo. I met him in the little cinderblock monastery that a UN agency had built in refugee days just beyond Sdok Kok Thom's southern outer wall. The Cambodian monks who were its original occupants were long gone, and Luang Poh Suwan Kanthathamo, a Thai, was now lord of the domain.

With him in his refuge were no other monks but quite a collection of Buddha images, facing east, like the ancient temple a few steps away. Among them was the black image that at its former place by the stone gate received the prayers of so many Thai villagers and refugees. With the ancient temple being returned to its original 11th century state, the modern image had found a new home here.

The priest was now the only person staying nights at Sdok Kok Thom, starlit as it was in ancient times. Sometimes after dark, he said, he heard sounds and smells coming from the temple courtyard. The first time it happened, shortly after he moved in, he called over the wall, thinking that there must be someone there. He laughed, at himself, on recalling this – he should have known what it really was. And there was the time a cobra slithered into his temple and lay next to him, keeping him company. But generally, he says, 'I don't want contact with the spirit. I go about my business and the spirit goes about its business.'

His business was Buddhist meditation. But he was also known all over Sakaew province as someone who could help with drug and alcohol addiction. The mobile phone clipped to his robes let people get in touch. Around Thailand, many priests had become part of this fight, which was focusing on a tidal wave of methamphetamines, known colloquially as *ya ba*, the drug that makes you crazy. Hidden labs far to the north in Thailand, Burma and Laos that used to process opium were now likely to be turning out the synthetic intoxicant.

On the afternoon that I visited, though, the monk was helping a man who had an older kind of addiction, alcoholism. His sister had brought him in. He'd been drinking hard for ten years, right up to the previous day, he explained to me in a whisper as he sat inside the temple. There was going to be an end to it, right here and now.

The monk wasn't listening just now. He was busy with a root from the forest. He was rubbing it over and over on a board propped in a

Luang Poh Suwan Kanthathamo, the sole monk at Sdok Kok Thom, 2009.

bowl of water. Fragments of root were collecting in the water, turning it brown. The alcoholic looked on, smiling nervously. Once he drank it down, he said, he would die if ever he touched alcohol again.

In another five minutes the monk was ready. First he sent the man forward to pray before the large golden Buddha that is the visual and spiritual focus of the temple's interior. The man did as told. On return, he was presented with the brown liquid. Down it went, chugged like beer at a dormitory party. Then priest and penitent knelt alongside each other, facing the image. 'Let this man resist alcohol and all other addictive drugs,' the priest said in the course of a prayer. Then it was over. 'You can go home.' The man did, though not before his sister, two friends and I received a blessing and a sprinkling of holy water.

It is possible that Luang Poh Suwan Kanthathamo lives on the exact same ground where Sadashiva's house stood, and that the modern monk, like those students at the nearby high school, is a blood descendent of the ancient Brahmin. Perhaps at some point archaeologists will find rotting posts in the ground and broken pottery that signal the location of the former abbot's residence. The question of bloodline will remain forever speculative. We have no record of the Brahmin clan after Sadashiva composed his text.

Which raises a question: does that lost trail have something to do with the inscription's existence?

The many scholars who've studied the text suggest quite a variety of answers to explain why the inscription was written. To some, it's mainly an unusually long-winded version of a standard Khmer inscriptional form, the marking of a new *linga's* consecration – toward the end, the text does mention the construction of Sdok Kok Thom and the placing of *lingas* there. The text can be seen also as a lengthy declaration of land rights, another common function for stone texts, and a warning of a curse on anyone who steals from the temple. Ang Chouleang, today Cambodia's pre-eminent specialist on inscriptions, cites explanations like those, but says that to him the text also feels like an outright boast. Sadashiva wanted to state in the most definitive, lasting way the myriad accomplishments of himself and his family and the exclusive rights of service that the palace had accorded the clan.

And perhaps there's something more as well. The fact that we hear nothing more about this family could be simply because later stone records did not survive through to present times. Or it could be that no further mentions have been found because the family no longer rated any mention. It had fallen from prominence.

Historians agree that the early 11th century was a time of great political upset in the Khmer Empire. The prince who fought his way to the throne as Suryavarman I, pushing aside two other kings in a lengthy civil war, was an outsider. He would have brought to the palace people who were either family or supporters who had thrown in their lot with him very early in his struggle, at great personal risk. The Brahmins of Sdok Kok Thom would appear to have been neither. They were consummate insiders of the old order, as the text so proudly documents, blue bloods ensconced in privilege for more than two centuries by that point. Some historians suggest that they may have declared their support for Suryavarman shortly before he became king, perhaps recognising the inevitable, and the inscription does describe them providing loyal service to him (it prudently makes no mention of two kings he vanquished). But perhaps the family's change of sides was viewed in the new court as opportunistic, too late.

With Suryavarman's accession, a slow decline appears to have set in for the family. Around this time, stones record another name in an increasingly prominent role in court, Kulke notes: the Saptadevakula family, which was connected by bonds of kinship to Suryavarman. One of its members, a man known by the honorary name Kavisvarapandita, was given responsibility for a major temple and *linga*. Later the family was headed by his nephew, the 'accomplished poet' Sankarapandita, who under the complex lineage of the time was also a maternal uncle of the king. The family appears to have continued to gain in standing under Suryavarman's successor, Udayadityavarman II. Its chief, Sankarapandita officiated at the golden *linga* atop the Baphuon, the mammoth mountain-temple that this new king built by the royal compound in Angkor.

Even without the change in dynasty, Sadashiva's family could have been in trouble. In his study, Kulke surmises that the clan's stock-in-trade, rites before the *devaraja*, was on the wane in Sadashiva's time. Another family was gaining the king's ear. In Kulke's view, Sadashiva probably wrote his testament in response to being passed over for the major honour of conducting rites at the Baphuon's summit.

So in 1052, the last year mentioned in the inscription, did Sadashiva come to the conclusion that his family's star was setting? That his marriage to the queen's sister and his new titles were intended as compensation for the pending loss of a two and a half century-old sinecure? We can imagine the shame and distress that such a demotion would have brought. Young members of the clan would have felt their futures had been snatched away. Old members would have complained that their long years of service had in the end counted for nothing.

I can picture Sadashiva, in the course of many trips to the capital over many years, putting up a fight to preserve the family's standing. But then one day, perhaps as he stands in a carved teak hall, having just stepped out of audience with a king who seems no longer so interested in his advice or the image that his family tends, he accepts that he is being eased out. As he travels back home, passing through forest and expanses of paddy land, he reaches a decision that the time for battling is passed.

But the clan will have the last word.

So, with 340 lines of immortal verse and prose, the priest gives to heaven, to king, to us, a poetic, spirited, firmly argued defence of his family's honour. See how ably we served! We were always there when king and realm needed us! Could heaven and earth have remained in harmony without our counsel, our grasp of the supernatural ways? Let it be known that if we no longer serve in this way, it is through no fault of our own. And let no one try to take our lands.

Why Sadashiva Wrote

We hear you, old priest. We hear you. You succeeded. Nine hundred years later, your family and its long, glorious run are not forgotten.

Sdok Kok Thom main sanctuary, 1979.

The Sdok Kok Thom inscription stored today in the Central Depository Unit of the National Museum of Thailand. Courtesy of M.L. Pattaratorn Chirapravati.

Postscript

We begin the drive at a bit after 9 a.m., in an old quarter of Bangkok near the Chao Phraya River. Morning rush hour traffic has thinned, but still holds us to a crawl. After ten minutes, I see relief ahead: the ramp to an elevated expressway. Thirty minutes of humming high speed follows, windows up, on a concrete artery that leads north from the city. Industrial plants, billboards and lighting pylons, globalisation's gifts to Thailand, whiz by. We leave the highway and pass by the shophouses of a satellite town. The road seems finally about to lead into rice land but instead delivers us to a large white institutional gate. Inside is what might be taken for a university campus, but it is a place where the Thai government stores history. The grounds are dominated by the newly built archives of King Bhumibol Adulyadej, who like all members of the Chakri Dynasty also bears the name Rama, one of many incarnations by which Vishnu takes pity on humankind and comes to earth to assist.

Our car passes the archive and stops at one of the smaller buildings on the grounds, the Central Depository Unit of the National Museum of Thailand. This is a home for collection items that officials have decided will not be on display to the public. It took the better part of a year, but I have finally gained access.

So it is that, at the tail end of my research, I come face to face with the thing that should have been my first stop.

Sadashiva's stone stands in a glass-walled room with perhaps two dozen other steles. There is no vortex of cosmic energy emanating from it. I make out no ghosts of abbot or stonecutter floating in its vicinity. Still, with its one and a half metre height and straight edges and profusion of words, it announces itself as apart from the rest, invested with some unperceivable essence. I feel a bit nervous. I lean close, respectfully, not too fast, to examine. It's all there, finally not in paper reproduction or photographic image or scholarly exegesis. The large letters of the Sanskrit verse, the Old Khmer writing that gets progressively smaller, the test letters carved at the base of one side. I dare to put out a finger. The stone is slightly sticky to the touch.

What of the fire of 1960? The stone's fragments were turned over to a renowned curator named Aporn Na Songkhla who spent years piecing them back together. Thus the stele underwent its own form of anastylosis, fallen elements raised to where they once had been. Alas, cracks are clearly visible. Here and there the surface now seems to be not of stone but some kind of repair compound that bridges gaps. On these areas, a restorer has painstakingly traced out the letters again in their precise original form, drawing on rubbings that were made before the fire. In my mind, none of this detracts. What I am seeing is merely the evidence of another chapter in a spectacular and not yet completed history.

But I do regret that the thing is hidden away. I hear and can think of varying explanations for why – there is no proper display venue for it, it is unsightly in its repaired state. Whatever the truth, as I write in 2010 the stone seems unlikely to go before the public any time soon. With tensions with Cambodia over border temples still strong, the Thai government might be reluctant to advertise that it possesses the most important record of ancient Cambodian history.

Hinduism has a concept called *Darshana*, in which worshippers not only offer prayers to an image but hear back from it. As I stand near the stone, my time with it almost up, I feel something resembling that. I'm in the presence of the priest because his words, his message to the ages, are right there before me. I have touched them. They are his communication with me. This is my story, they say. Because of them, I continue to exist.

At the top of the first side, his message opens as it has for nearly a millennium.

Praise be to Shiva!
Whose nature is proclaimed wordlessly yet thunderously,
By the subtle soul-life of the body,
A nature that reaches everywhere,
And quickens the senses of all living beings.

Postscript

A scene representing the Churning of the Sea of Milk brought back to France by Aymonier on one of his expeditions. Today it is housed at the Musée Guimet.

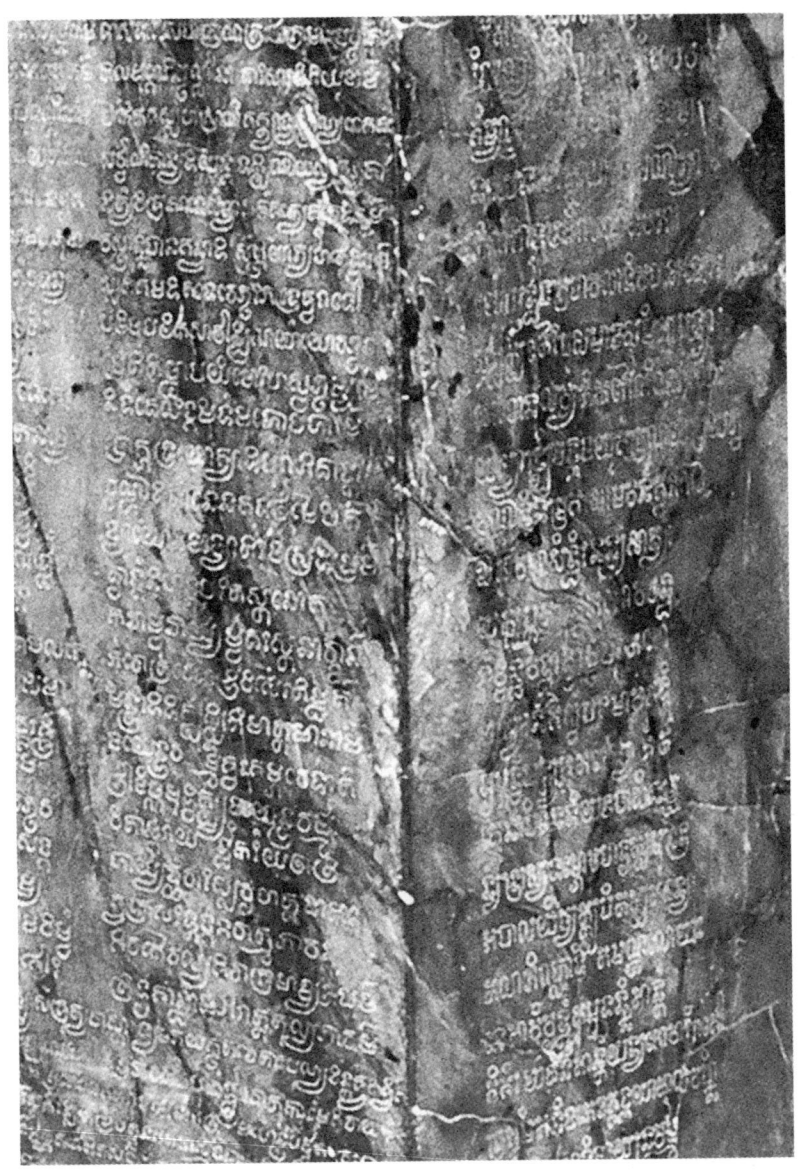

Detail of the Sdok Kok Thom inscription.
Courtesy of M.L. Pattaratorn Chirapravati.

The Sdok Kok Thom Inscription: Full Translation

To read the Sdok Kok Thom inscription, first clear your mind of any clutter. Be willing to take time, to linger over phrases that catch your fancy, to reread and ponder. The thousand-year-old words of the presumed author, the Brahmin priest Sadashiva, decline to reveal their meanings right away. This is due in part to a prose style and cultural literacy far removed from today's: The priest alludes at every turn to the faith, myth and metaphor of the times. Characters human and divine appear under multiple names, titles are repeated *ad infinitum*. Narrative transitions, trusty helpmates in modern writing, are unknown. And some portions of the text simply remain a mystery, despite more than a century of scrutiny by a very talented corps of scholars.

But be patient. Press forward. The language is beautiful. Into your consciousness will flow the ambiance of Southeast Asia of a millennium ago. You will begin to appreciate the devotion to the Hindu cosmos that dominated regal life in that age. You'll taste also of very real-world events of military conquest and the construction of new towns and villages. You will meet great personages of the day and be party to elaborate thank-you notes for royal gifts. You will learn details of the labour and liturgical implements required to keep a medium-sized 11th century Hindu temple in operation.

In 2005, Dr. Chhany Sak-Humphry, professor of Hawaiian and Indo-Pacific languages and literatures at the University of Hawaii, with assistance from Dr. Philip N. Jenner, professor emeritus of Indo-Pacific languages at that university, published an English translation of the inscription through Cambodia's Buddhist Institute. It is reproduced here by the kind permission of Dr. Sak-Humphry, with some minor editing aimed at helping the novice reader. Accent marks in the Roman script transliteration of Sanskrit and Old Khmer proper names, for instance, have been removed. Certain words that in the 2005 translation were left in the original tongue and analysed in footnotes have here been rendered in English deemed closest to their meanings. At the same time, a few Sanskrit words which have entered English with close to their original definitions, such as ashram and guru, are left in the original.

Here, then, is the chronicle, with section introductions written by me.

John Burgess.

Sanskrit Text

Sadashiva opens the inscription with praise to the god whose name he bears and to whom the temple was dedicated, Shiva, the Hindu trinity's first among equals (in the priest's era and culture, at least). In this passage he is also called the Benefactor, and later on in the text he will appear under half a dozen different appellations. His holy consort is Parvati, goddess of fortune and beauty. Shiva has many attributes. One of his best known is mentioned here, a third eye, centered in his forehead.

The verse goes quickly on to offer homage to the two other members of the Trinity and their consorts: Brahma, here called the Creator, whose consort sometimes bears the name Bharati. Vishnu, the third member of the Trinity, is not immediately mentioned by name, but his presence is signaled by allusion to his consort Lakshmi and a great jewel with which he is associated.

> *Praise be to Shiva! Whose nature is proclaimed wordlessly yet thunderously by the subtle soul-life of his body – which reaches everywhere and quickens the senses of all living beings.*

> *May the Benefactor protect the universe, he who through three eyes has a pure and perfect vision of the true nature of the unveiled true self.*

> *May the Creator preserve you – he who bears a vessel of ambrosia, a crystal vessel shining as the moon, the deep source of that ocean of nectar which is his compassion for the worlds.*

> *May Lakshmi's Lord preserve you – he on whose breast the seated Lakshmi seems to say: 'As even those of stable nature need support, so I, of unstable nature, rest here on the Kaustubha jewel'.*

Having praised heaven, the inscription now descends earthward to acknowledge the highest-ranking human of the time, King Udayadityavarman II, who ascended the throne around the year 1050 AD. The king's name means 'rising sun,' hence the many allusions to light. He is depicted as the ideal ruler, drawing obeisance even from other kings who, metaphorically at least, dare touch only his feet, the least sacred part of his body. He can cause subjects to bloom to their fullest. He is said to have been placed on the throne by Brahma. In quick succession, the verse alludes again to all three of the Trinity consorts. Himalaya, a deification of the Indian mountains of the same name, is the father of Parvati, Shiva's consort.

> There was once a sovereign of the world whose feet were clasped by all kings, whose part it was to cause the hearts of men to unfold as lotuses, who dispelled all gloom, and who by reason of his splendor was named Udayaditya.
>
> 'Love, whom I brought into being with the wisdom of my supreme brilliancy, has become fuel for the fire in Hara's [Shiva's] eye.' So saying, Brahma (I fancy) with his ambrosial beams made manifest a god of love, whom he raised to sovereign power.
>
> 'Who am I, who like Himalaya's daughter embraces half of my gentle lord's body?' So wonders Lakshmi, as if outside herself, as she closely clasps his body, fair as that of Love.
>
> Intent to hear from his very mouths this four-mouthed Brahma (whose self, for the world's good, is graced with charity and like royal virtues), the devoted Bharat clings to his side and, taking him for the Creator, with him fixes her abode.

The verse now returns to praising the king's many virtues. He is said to have a glorious *mandala*, a word that today refers most commonly to the elaborate circular symbols used in Buddhist and Hindu prayer. The term can also allude to the cosmos in general. The egg of Hiranyagarbha is the golden womb from which the universe was created.

> His mind was trained in all accomplishments, the arts as well as others. Indeed, it is to count his excellences that the delighted Creator still today employs a rosary, the telling of which is but a pretense.
>
> Quick to recognise forbidden women, he would look upon another's wife unlustfully or as poison. Yet did he enjoy in other ways the ever sensual pleasures of those Wives of Duty: Glory, Faith, Compassion, and Steadfastness.
>
> The earth (prey to suffering, exhausted, bewildered, miserable) sought refuge in his royal vigor of gentle brilliance, whereby with peerless activity he restored it to perfect felicity.
>
> The mandala of his glory (vast, shading the Three Worlds, covered with praises as with blossoms) sank its roots into the hearts of men as if in fear of cracking the egg of Hiranyagarbha.

As a teacher exhorts his disciples, or a father his children, even so (with eyes fixed on his duty) he strove tirelessly for the protection and prosperity of his people.

We are told now that the king had great skills as a warrior, another of the virtues expected of Khmer monarchs.

In battle he bore a sword red with the blood of enemy kings it had slain, which cast a dazzling light in all directions like a ravishing red lotus issued from its calyx which by sheer strength of arm he had ripped from the hair of the Goddess of War.

In this war-sacrifice His Majesty's roaring fire (fed by the fuel of hostile troops, fanned by the wind of his mighty arm) must surely have scorched the earth to such degree that it was compelled to take refuge in the moon's disk in the form of a gazelle.

His lotus feet proclaimed his affection for his friends, for the host of kings bowing down before him were reflected in the gems of his nails, causing them to enter into him by force of his good will for their devotion.

Miraculous was this king's potency: his magic power, beyond the range of others, may be judged by a sacrifice he once celebrated which bound Indra and the other gods forevermore.

Vishnu's body was engulfed in the rush of smoke spewing from the fire of his relentlessly celebrated sacrifices, which constantly invaded that god's abode – whence it happens that Vishnu is black to this day.

Having no fear of them, he spared hundreds of proud but distant foes, which kept him not from dispatching lesser pursuers close at hand: the Six Enemies.

How could Vishnu, had he been alert as protector, have slept at ease on the surface of the sea? This king sought to protect men by binding our wounds with the elixir of the wisdom of the Manavas.

He gladdened his realm by his accomplishments. He emitted beams of light marked by mercy. He made lotuses to open. Ravishing, he was rightly hailed with the title of Moon.

To Sanskrit specialists, the preceding verse is one of the tougher to translate because many of its words have double meanings alluding to light and brightness. The 'beams of light' sentence, for instance, has also been translated as 'He levied taxes that were imbued with lenience.'

In the following verse, the king is associated with the goddess Kali, whose attribute of burning and luminosity continues the theme of light.

> *His glory at sea, ever bright with Kali's burning, utterly cooled his subjects amidst the heat of conflagration. Kali's fire, fearful of having its ardor quenched by his, went into hiding in the deep of the Creator's egg.*

Now comes the introduction of Sadashiva, here appearing under one of his many honorific names, Jayendravarman. There is immediate stress on the purity of his maternal line. Bloodline among the Brahmin elite was commonly by the mother's side, that is, succession often went to the son of the sister of a great priest, not to the son of the priest, as is specified repeatedly in the inscription.

> *He had a guru commanding high respect for his understanding: the celebrated Holy Jayendravarman, born of a high-ranking family of irreproachable name.*

> *His maternal line – the sundry accomplishments of which had earlier been won by the Sun's descendants without being thereby diminished – was as an earthly embodiment of the Moon for the world's good.*

The narrative now jumps back more than two centuries for an initial telling of the founding of the empire. The first member of the priestly line, Shivakaivalya, is introduced. So too is another Brahmin, Hiranyadama, who seems not to have been part of the family but had a crucial role in establishing its place in palace ritual. The four Hindu treatises that are cited have only been partially identified. Tumburu is the chief of a class of nature spirits known as *gandhavas*.

> *The monarch Jayavarman [II], who had fixed his residence on the summit of Mount Mahendra, had as master a sage whose feet were saluted by the noblest heads, who was called Shivakaivalya.*

> *That great and surpassingly wise Brahmin Hiranyadama, having come as a merciful Brahma, respectfully exhibited before this king a magic power possessed by no other.*
>
> *At the king's behest this Brahmin imparted magic power and its practices to this chaplain [Shivakaivalya], whose pure heart, for the increase of his power, was intent upon the good.*
>
> *As if by magic means this Brahmin [Hiranyadama] taught him [Shivakaivalya] the treatises entitled Shirashcheda, Vinashikha, Sammoha, and Nayottara, those four faces of Tumburu.*

In the following verse comes the word – *devaraja* – that was to cause so much debate, so much second-guessing among historians (see Chapter X). Early French interpretations that it referred to a king turned into a god have given way to a consensus view that it was a holy image or object, the tending of which was the priestly family's main ritual function.

> *This Brahmin, having distilled the essence of these treatises with understanding and experience in mysteries, established for the world's prosperity the magic rites which bear the name of devaraja.*
>
> *To give the world unmixed felicity, the king appointed to this worship, source of a power hoard, this sage together with the chief Brahmin.*

The story continues on the stele's second side. Sadashiva declares that his family alone, pure in maternal blood, has the authority to tend the *devaraja*.

> *May no others but an ascetic born of women of this maternal line and gifted with learning and vigor be priests of this worship!' Such was the injunction of the royal Brahmin.*

Now begins a catalogue of lands that the family has acquired. Often the first order of business was setting up a *linga*, a stone shaft that contained the essence of Shiva and was the focus of worship in temples of the time. Ian Mabbett and David Chandler have dubbed the process described here as 'ecclesiastical colonisation.' The priestly family acquires land, then develops and settles it, often bringing in relatives to populate new villages and towns, or at least to serve as the local gentry.

> On land in the territory of Indrapura, earlier given his line by the prince of Bhavapura, this Brahmin kept a most puissant Sharvalinga [Shivalinga], set up in the thriving town of Bhadrayogi.
>
> Obtaining from the sovereign land in the territory of Purvadisa, he founded there a town named Kuti and settled his family in it.
>
> Obtaining from the sovereign land in the vicinity of Amarendrapura, he founded on it a town named Bhavalaya and there set up a linga.
>
> Chaplain to this king's son, the monarch Jayavarman [III], was Sukshmavindu, son of Shivakaivalya's sister and first of sages in point of wisdom.
>
> From this same king, Rudracarya, younger brother of Shivakaivalya, secured a mountain here in the territory of Adripada.
>
> Having founded a village and set up the linga of Ishvara [Shiva] by due rites, this sage named this mountain Bhadragiri.
>
> Chaplain to King Sri Indravarman was Vamashiva, able younger brother of Sukshmavindu, guru to Sri Yashovardhana [the crown prince].

An ashram – Shivashrama is its name – is established, with two men taking charge of it. They adopt the name of the retreat as their own name. Early French scholars attempted unsuccessfully to identify the location of Shivashrama, some of them becoming certain that it was the Bayon temple. In fact, that temple in Angkor Thom city was built almost three centuries after the events being described here. Shivasrama remains unlocated, like many of the places mentioned in the text.

> This Vamashiva, a disciple of this king's guru Shivasoma, was like a river of knowledge of the true self given physical form.
>
> Having built the Shivasrama and being of the same mind as his disciple, Shivasoma set up the linga of Shiva there.
>
> Both men were called Shivasrama, and on Shivasoma's death Vamashiva took charge of the Shivashrama.
>
> When Sri Yashovardhana became king under the name Sri Yashovarman, the able Vamashiva continued as his guru.

> By the King's order he set up a linga on Sri Yashodharagiri, a mountain equal in beauty to the King of Mountains.
>
> As his lord's gracious gift, the wise spiritual preceptor received the land of Jayapattani, hard by Bhadragiri.
>
> On this land the monarch founded a town called Bhadrapattana and there set up the linga of Ishvara as a gift of respect to the guru.

Next comes a compilation of gifts from a king to the family, one of several lists that the inscription will give. The meaning of the word 'karanka' is not understood; 'desha' and 'grama' appear to be administrative units. The king is meanwhile recounted as taking a common initiative of Khmer monarchs, the endowing of a temple to a particular god, with specific agricultural lands being assigned to support it.

> He gave him things for his use: karanka, ewers, and the like, abundant riches such as cows and two hundred male and female slaves.
>
> In the desha of Amoghapura, the munificent sovereign, best of givers, assigned to Sambhu [Shiva] lands in Ganeshvara with their boundaries fixed.
>
> On land in Bhadrapattana, the noble-minded Shivashrama founded the town of Bhadravasa and there installed an image of Sarasvati [another name for the wife of Brahma].
>
> From this same king, Hiranyaruci, the supremely wise younger brother of the two Shivashramas, obtained the land called Vamshahrada.
>
> In the town he founded there this prince of able men, of rich intelligence, set up by due rite the linga of Ishvara [Shiva] for his family's prosperity.
>
> These two personages sent for three of their sister's daughters from the grama of Kuti and settled two in Vamshahrada, one in Bhadrapattana.
>
> Kumarasvamin, son of the Shivashrama's sister, was chaplain to King Sri Harshavarman and, later, to [King] Sri Ishanavarman.

The Sdok Kok Thom Inscription

Parashara is the reputed author of the great Hindu text the *Rig Veda*. In the following passage, the new family head, Kumarasvamin, names a town after him and is compared in wisdom to his son.

This seer, this spiritual guide endowed with the sovereign intelligence of Parashara's son, founded the town of Parashara on land in Vamshahrada.

The son of the Shivashramas' sister's daughter, Isanamurti by name, of flawless intelligence, was chaplain to Sri Jayavarman [IV].

Receiving land by this king's favor, this illustrious wise man founded the town of Khmvan out of devotion to the Lord of the Three Worlds.

This new chaplain is likened to Angirasa, a god who functions as chaplain to the gods and frequently intercedes in the human world.

Chaplain to King Hashavarman was Atmashiva, son of Ishanamurti's sister, who was gifted with the sovereign intelligence of Angirasa.

As chaplain to Rajendravarman, he founded the towns of Shantipura, and Katukapura and Brahmapura on lands of Vamshahrada.

There, in each of these three grama, he set up images of Hara [Shiva], Vishnu and Sarasvati for the sake of well being.

Chaplain to Jayavarman was the intelligent son of the daughter of Atmashiva's sister, Shivacarya of blessed aptitudes.

During the reign of Suryavarman [I], he set up by due rite images of Harihara [a deity that combines Shiva and Vishnu] and Sarasvati in Bhadrapattana.

Residing in the royal city, these excellent learned men of high intelligence, worthy of the homage and the company of kings, thus celebrated punctually, strictly, zealously the daily service to the devaraja *and none other.*

The story has arrived back at contemporary times, with Sadashiva becoming family head.

A scion of this able, blessed female line was renowned under the name of Sadashiva, son of Shivacarya's sister, whose noble heart was ever Shiva's throne.

Molded by practice to the worship of the devaraja *and upholding the traditions of his illustrious line, he was family priest to the sovereign Suryavarman and among all family priests was venerated for his character.*

Ever and utterly transported by the ambrosia of his ceaseless worship, and relinquishing all his own powers, Sharva [Shiva] entered his unflawed heart without impediment.

'In what refuge might I dwell forevermore where the darkness of anger and other passions does not also dwell?' So saying, Dharma in the hope of escaping darkness took up residence in his most worthy heart, rich in prudence.

He was the storehouse of that wealth which is Dharma; he was that jewel's issue which is good conduct; he was the ocean of that river which is propriety; he was the soil of that seed which is self-regard.

Tirelessly reciting the text of treatises to be learned, he then imparted them to others. Each day he offered up a garland of eight kinds of flowers to gladden the hearts of fire and Astatanu [Shiva].

The fully opened lotus of his heart was fragrant with the Sabdartha and other treatises, while the questions of his adversaries (so many bees driven by the wind of his learning) found no easy resting place with him.

Refuge of the Supreme Spirit, treasure of depth and other qualities, most beneficent, glistening as a bright jewel, he bore within himself the likeness of the sea.

Selflessly could he give wealth in jewels and the like to needy, deserving Brahmin, yet artfully did he take unto himself their minds' hidden riches through a covetousness surpassing that of other men.

His eyes were drawn to good conduct, not to the flesh, for he was devoid of all thoughts of Love. Merit to be gained was what excited him, not sound or other objects of the senses.

Pre-eminent in beauty, power, glory, knowledge, virtue, deeds, and merit, he was without pride. He knew music; he had learned the arts (mechanics, astronomy, medicine, and others); he was master of ritual.

Experienced, wise, wealthy, renowned for his goodness toward all and for his proficiency in music, ceaselessly did he delight the hearts of those attending him by the five bonds bred of courtesy.

[King] Sri Suryavarman bade him return, following the prescribed rites, to the condition of householder and gave him to wife, in the presence of fire and Brahmins, the sister of [Queen] Sri Viralakshmi.

Sadashiva receives a new honorific, which translates roughly as Victorious-Indra-Wiseman. The priest is also assigned a new royal position in which he keeps busy as a sort of construction manager and developer.

Vanquisher of poets, prince of talented men, most proficient of scholars, for his attachment to the king he received the name, well deserved and full of sweet promise, of Holy Jayendrapandita.

His heart full of devotion to his lord Sri Suryavarman, enjoyer of wondrous felicity, he received, together with the office of Inspector of Sacrifices, a golden palanquin and other gifts.

Repository of great might, in the desha *of Bhadrayogi and other places in Indrapuri and elsewhere he constructed pools and the like as fruitful works of piety toward the deities there established, and set up there a Sharvalinga [Shivalinga] and other deities.*

Royal chaplain, chief of ascetics having custody of the deity, housemaster endowed with morality, learning, and abilities, he was devoted to duty.

At Bhadrapattana he set up by due rite a linga and two images, and built a temple pinnacle provided with a limonite wall.

Having given these three deities all that they required, slaves and the like, he built a channel and a pool there for the region's prosperity.

> At Bhadravasa he amassed and gave to Sarasvati a great fortune, and this man of practical turn built a pool as well as a park and ditch.
>
> To the god of Bhadradri he consecrated an ashram, enlarged by his own efforts; he filled its stables with cows and built a channel and waterway.
>
> At Vamshahrada he gave to the god all the wealth he had laid up; he built an oblong pond, a ditch, and a pool for the prosperity of the land.
>
> In the desha of Amoghapura he received a certain piece of land called Camka from Sri Suryavarman, for the benefit of his female line.
>
> He [also] acquired a piece of land in the desha of Amoghapura to the east of the pool of Maharatha and on the other side of the river.
>
> All these lands acquired by gift or purchase he donated to the abbot of Vamshahrada and his family.
>
> On family land at Nagasundara in Amoghapura he founded a rich village, which he gave to the Shambu [Shiva] at Bhadrapattana.
>
> In Brahmapura, after setting up an image of Sarasvati, he gave it slaves and constructed a bhanga, a pool, and a waterway.
>
> In the town of Kuti, after erecting a temple, he set up therein the linga of Isha [Shiva] of his own making and more than once endowed it with chattels, slaves, and the like.
>
> Suing Suryavarman for abandoned land at Bahuyuddha in the town of Jen Dnap, and taking possession of it, he bestowed it on the Isha [Shiva] of Kuti and on his family.
>
> He was a kinsman on his father's side of Vagindrakavi, at whose feet [he had studied] the Shabdashastra and other texts.
>
> Making various endowments for his master, he built an ashram filled with riches given as respectful gifts to a guru, dedicating it to Shiva.

Sadashiva now receives yet another title, beginning with 'Dust of the Feet,' a sign that even dust is holy when associated with a

The Sdok Kok Thom Inscription

man of this piety. Like everyone in the Khmer empire, Sadashiva went barefoot, so his feet were indeed often dust-coated. 'Varman' is a suffix used by kings and other members of the elite. It roughly means protector.

> *This eminent man, who enjoyed uncommon power by reason of his station as guru to [King] Udayadityavarman [II], received a name beginning with 'Dust of the Feet' and ending in 'varman,' a glorious name achieved by no one else.*

Again, the inscription assumes deep knowledge of Hindu lore and history. Here the guru is compared to two sages who instruct gods or lofty humans. The Candra may be a dynasty that ruled in India at roughly the same time as the inscription was written.

> *Respected by wisemen for his intelligence, he instructed Udayaditya as Atri or Kashyapa imparted political science and all other subjects to Indra or Candra.*

Sadashiva begins another reckoning of gifts provided by the king. The meaning of some words that appear to refer to implements and units of measure are not understood; they have been left untranslated in the text below. Elippsises mark the few spots on the stone where words are illegible.

> *The king of kings, having learned the principles of good conduct, ...content, consecrated according to rite and most learned, venerated him and honored him with magnificent gifts.*

> *This king took pleasure thenceforth in lavishing on him eagerly and in due form, and in his own [Sadashiva's] mansion the most agreeable marks of distinction – wondrous banquets and the like.*

> *This [mansion] was embellished with the most seductive images of carved stone, covered with a series of arrangements ornamented with women. How could one dream of speaking of other beauty?*

> *[Among the King's gifts were] a magnificent head ornament, ear-rings, armlets, necklaces and the like, [other] ornaments, a hundred finger rings;*

> *Gold vessels, a fly-whisk, a shining seat, a gold palanquin with a three-headed serpent, a gleaming goblet;*

Heaps of a thousand gems such as rubies, gold ewers and drinking vessels, bowls, and basins for washing the hands;

Water vessels, drinking cups, [other] cups, hand-basins and cuspidors, gold pitchers, and various other fine things;

Copper vessels and gold pitchers...set out by types, each in the thousands;

A thousand vessels of tin...a hundred articles of raiment worthy of a king, a hundred mantles;

Four thousand monk's habits and four hundred [other] garments, three catties of camphor, one catty of musk;

Five triple-bushels of nutmeg, ten triple-bushels of cubeb pepper, and indeed twenty triple-bushels of black pepper;

One tael of the spice asafœtida, one triple-bushel of cumin, twenty-five triple-bushels of dried ginger;

Two triple-bushels of cumin-seed, a triple-bushel of Thespesia populneoides cuttings, a triple-bushel each of long pepper and costus root;

One bhara *of sandal resin, the same amount of eaglewood, five catties each of styrax and sal ammoniac mineral;*

A double drona of aromatic onyx, five triple-bushels of cardamom, a thousand balls of crushed cloves;

Two hundred spirited, well paced elephants, male and female, with temple armor and bells, carrying mahouts with goads;

A hundred steeds, mostly black-eared stallions, with their handlers and their bridles, drawing chariots and jangling their belled harnesses;

Five hundred humped cows with their calves, two hundred and fifty buffaloes, a hundred sheep, a hundred swine;

A hundred women splendidly bejewelled, with trantridali *and the like, and with a hundred sweet-sounding lutes and flutes;*

Half a hundred instrumentalists with brass cymbals, drums and the like; three villages complete with a thousand male and female slaves;

> *Four hundred wagons hitched to strong draught animals, filled with sesame and beans, and managed by diligent drivers;*
>
> *Of good hatchets, khurddala and well hafted axes a thousand each; spears and like, and arrows in great number;*
>
> *Rice by the thousand [measures]; indeed, grain by tens of thousands. All this was given to this man as the sovereign's gift.*
>
> *Such was the tally of the gifts offered by the king to this man on a single occasion. With such constant munificence, how could anyone know their number?*
>
> *Ever reverenced by the fervent king, daily did he receive marks of honor in the form of raiment, food, drink, perfumes, and the like.*
>
> *Unceasingly did this bountiful master [Sadashiva] give unto Bhadreshvara and other deities a mass of wealth in the form of jewels and artifacts of gold and other substances. Devoted solely to the well being of others, he built houses and ponds along roadways for the benefit of processions of wayfarers.*

For the first time, the area in which Sdok Kok Thom has been built is mentioned, by its Sanskrit name Bhadraniketana, Blessed Edifice of Worship.

> *On behalf of his guru, who desired to make an endowment on land of his own, the magnanimous King set up a linga in the locality called Bhadraniketana as his lavish gift.*
>
> *In addition to this Bhadraniketana, which has the same first element as Bhadrayogi of old and other towns, he [the king] showered good and precious stones as well as the best of elephants and a multitude of horses and the like on this linga and voiced this prayer for him [his guru]:*
>
> *'May this Sharva-Jayendravarman, with honor and success, dispel the darkness by projecting all around himself the radiance of his constant splendor until the extinction of living things!'*

The following list of planetary positions is a common way in Khmer inscriptions of giving a precise time when a particular event occurred.

> *The sun and other planets being in Aquarius, Virgo, Libra, Aquarius, Aquarius, Pisces, Aquarius, Aquarius and Pisces, the horoscope being in Sagittarius, Bhava [Shiva] hath risen here in the year marked by the [nine] orifices, the [seven] mountains, and the [four] Vedas.*
>
> *Out of devotion to the lord Shambhu [Shiva] Jayendravarman [Sadashiva], King Udayaditya, having determined its extent and laid down boundary markers all around, gave him lands extending eastward and towards the other cardinal points beyond his domain.*
>
> *Seeing the King illumined with great joy, Jayendravarman evinced an attachment to him, as did Atri [another author of Vedic hymns], which safeguarded him from all impediments.*

Sadashiva now speaks of the temple itself. The 'great deep pool' is presumably the *baray*, or holy reservoir, that lies just east of the temple. He offers the charming detail that swans glided across its waters. He records that the temple included images honouring the two great Brahmins of the court of the founder king Jayavarman II: the first of the priestly bloodline Shivakaivalya and Hiranyadama, the man who imparted the 'magic' of the *devaraja*. The Sanskrit portion of the inscription then closes with a warning against thieves – the words stand alone at the top of the stele's Side D, which otherwise contains only Old Khmer words. As Khmer inscription curses go, this one is relatively simple and straightforward.

> *This great deep pool – whose clear waters excite the lust of swans among the lotuses and charm by his liberality to Brahmins and others – was made by him to epitomise his mission as protector.*
>
> *This well disposed man erected by due rite the images called the Shivakaivalya-Shivashrama, equal in majesty to Brahma, and Shiva-Vishnu, together with an image of Hiranyadama.*
>
> *Whoso views this ideal abode, foremost on earth, or merely hears it spoken of, his mind is at rest, his soul is sanctified. What is Shiva's brings instant misfortune to him who would take it unto himself. He who makes gifts to Shiva is enriched in all forms of prosperity.*
>
> *He who by word, thought or deed shall harm what is Shiva's – be it land, gold, silver, slaves or other things – shall undergo atonement in the two worlds.*

Old Khmer Text

From the start, the Old Khmer section gives a more direct reporting of facts, names and numbers, as is usual in inscriptions in this common language of the era. There is no opening paean to Heaven; Sadashiva dives right into the story of how two and a half centuries earlier the priestly line received a special ritual mandate from Jayavarman II as the conqueror strived to create an empire from feuding principalities.

The text refers to kings by their posthumous names, another common pattern in Old Khmer texts. The term *'kamraten jagata'*, translated here as Sovereign High Lord of the World, is taken to be the Old Khmer counterpart to the Sanskrit *devaraja*. The word *kamraten* is the word that the linguist Étienne Aymonier was puzzling over in 1879 when he had his epiphany that Khmer inscriptions, though written with a single alphabet, were often in two languages, Sanskrit and Old Khmer, a precursor to modern Cambodian (see Chapter V).

When His Majesty Parameshvara [Jayavarman II] set up the Sovereign High Lord of the World in the royal city of Mahendraparvata, he appointed members of a line among the inhabitants of Stuk Ransi in Bhadrapattana to be the ones to serve thereafter as officiants to that divinity. An edict excluded all save members of this line from officiating before it. Following is the origin of the said line.

The family in Aninditapura had its roots in Shatagrama commune. The prince of Bhavapura had granted it lands in the territory of Indrapura. The family founded Bhadrayogi commune, settled in it, and set up a holy Shivalinga there. When His Majesty Parameshvara came from Java to reign in the royal city of Indrapura the August Shivakaivalya, the family's learned patriarch, was serving as his guru and held the post of royal chaplain to His Majesty. When the sovereign quit Indrapura, the August Shivakaivalya came with him as a member of the College of Sacrifice in the royal service. His Majesty had him bring his family with him, females as well as males. Once they had reached the territory of Purvadisha, His Majesty bade give them land on which to found the commune of Kuti and settle them in it.

While His Majesty Parameshvara reigned in the royal city of Hariharalaya, the August Shivakaivalya dwelt there as well. At

> His Majesty's bidding, the family was reassigned to the Corps of Pages. When His Majesty founded the royal city of Amarendrapura the August Shivakaivalya took up residence there as well and served him. He petitioned His Majesty for a tract of land near Amarendrapura and founded on it the commune of Bhavalaya. He brought some of his family from Kuti commune and had them settle there, giving them over to a Brahmin named Gangadhara. In addition, he set up a holy Shivalinga and assigned slaves to it. When His Majesty left Amarendrapura to reign on Mount Mahendra the August Shivakaivalya likewise went and took up residence there, serving His Majesty as before.

The tale of the family's early assignment to a role of honour in court religious life is told again. There is mention of Kambujadesa, which in later times would mean the Cambodian state but during this period perhaps alludes more to a nascent Cambodian ethnicity, a people unified by culture but not yet by a single state. The Sovereign of the World, or *cakravartin*, is the king in his role as head of an empire. This is not to be confused with Sovereign High Lord of the World, which is the image or holy object that was focus of the family's religious service.

The word here rendered as 'Java' has been subjected to almost as much analysis as *devaraja* (see Chapter IX). Early scholars thought that it meant the island Java and speculated that the young Jayavarman had been taken there as a hostage. More recent scholarship suggests it meant any place under influence of the Hindu kingdom centered on Java, or that it might refer not to Java at all but to the land of the Cham people in modern-day southern Vietnam.

> When the Brahmin Hiranyadama, proficient in the lore of magic power, came from Janapada in response to His Majesty's having invited him to perform a sublime rite which would release Kambujadesa from being any longer subject to Java and which would enable the sole High Lords of Earth to be Sovereign of the World, this Hiranyadama celebrated a rite from the Vinashikha and established the Sovereign High Lord of the World.

> The said Brahmin instructed the August Shivakaivalya in the holy Vinashikha, the Nayottara, the Sammoha and the Shirashcheda. These he recited in their entirety that the august priest might write them down so that they could be imparted to him by this means. He then directed the August Shivakaivalya to be the one to perform

the rite before the Sovereign High Lord of the World. His Majesty and the Brahmin Hiranyadama issued an edict naming the line of Shivakaivalya as the one to officiate before the divinity and prohibiting others from doing so. As royal chaplain, Shivakaivalya assigned sundry members of the family to officiate.

When His Majesty Parameshvara returned to reign in Hariharalaya, the Sovereign High Lord of the World was brought with him. The August Shivakaivalya and various members of his family continued to officiate as before. Shivakaivalya died during that same reign. His Majesty Parameshvara departed this life in the royal city of Hariharalaya.

The location of the Sovereign High Lord of the World changed with the royal city in which the High Lord of Earth resided, and was taken with him. It is this divinity that safeguarded the realm from that time on.

During the reign of His Majesty Vishnuloka [Jayavarman III, son of Jayavarman II] the Sovereign High Lord of the World remained in Hariharalaya. A nephew of the August Shivakaivalya who was named the August Sukshmavindu served as chaplain to the divinity. Various members of the family officiated before it as well.

This Sukshmavindu moved the members of his family who were in Bhavalaya and settled them all together in Kuti commune.

The August Rudracarya, a younger brother of Shivakaivalya, went out and entered holy orders in the territory of Jen Vnam on a hill named Thko. He petitioned His Majesty Vishnuloka for this hill and its surrounding lands, laid out a commune and set up an image in it, naming the hill Bhadragiri.

During the reign of His Majesty Ishvaraloka [Indravarman I], the Sovereign High Lord of the World remained in Hariharalaya, and various members of the family continued to officiate before it as before. The August Vamashiva, grandson of the August Shivakaivalya, served as preceptor to His Majesty. The sovereign gave him to His Majesty Paramashivaloka [King Yasovarman] when the latter was still young and had him instruct him. This August Vamashiva had been a disciple of the August Shivasoma, who had been His Majesty's guru.

> *Shivasoma and Vamashiva together founded the Shivashrama and were the ones who set up the image there. Shivasoma was known as the Elder High Lord of the Shivashrama while Vamashiva was known as the Younger High Lord of the Shivashrama.*
>
> *When Shivasoma died, Vamashiva was the head of that facility, and continued to be known as the High Lord of the Shivashrama as before. When His Majesty Paramashivaloka appointed Vamashiva, still known as the High Lord of the Shivashrama, to serve as royal spiritual preceptor, he became custodian of the property as well as the images which had been set up by his line in Indrapura down to Bhavalaya commune near Amarendrapura, in Kuti commune in Purvadisha, and in Bhadragiri commune in Jen Vnam. Members of the family continued to officiate before the Sovereign High Lord of the World as before.*

The following passage depicts the relocation of the capital to the area where Angkor Wat and Angkor Thom city now stand. The term 'Central Mountain' confused early French scholars—they were convinced that it referred to the Bayon temple, which stands at the central point within Angkor Thom's walls (see Chapter XI). Until the 1930s, experts erroneously considered the Bayon and temples of similar style to be Angkor's oldest, built around 900 AD, though in fact they are among its newest and date to roughly three centuries later.

> *When His Majesty Paramashivaloka founded the royal city of Yashodharapura, he brought the Sovereign High Lord of the World from Hariharalaya and installed it in the new royal city. When His Majesty raised the Central Mountain, Vamashiva, High Lord of the Shivashrama, set up a holy linga in its center. After this, he established the offices of the royal service.*

Now begins more acquisition and development of land. The inscription uses the term '*vroh*', a unit of land whose size remains unknown, and for that reason the word is left untranslated here.

> *Informing His Majesty that he desired to set up another image, he petitioned for land on which to do so. When the line's patriarch, the August Rudracarya, came and met with Vamashiva to advise him that there were ravaged lands belonging to the order in Vijayapattana adjacent to Bhadragiri (which belonged to Rudracarya and his folk), this Rudracarya bade him petition for that land.*

Vamashiva did petition Paramashivaloka for it, and founded on it Bhadrapattana commune and Bhadravasa commune. His Majesty gave him a holy linga two cubits high which had been set up on the Central Mountain but was no longer needed, and this was set up in Bhadrapattana. An image of Bhagavati was set up in Bhadravasa commune, part of the lands of Bhadrapattana. His Majesty also gave him things for that divinity's use, in particular a vessel, a metal vessel, cult objects, and all manner of other costly things, all by way of a holy gift to Vamashiva, and two hundred slaves. He [also] gave two hundred vroh of riceland in Ganeshvara in the district of Amoghapura, which was divided up and given to Stuk Ransi as well.

His Majesty Paramashivaloka directed a certain cleric named the August Shika, a disciple of Vamashiva, to join the Royal Service. The sovereign bade him go out and organise the [new] commune of Bhadrapattana and set up an image in it, employing two clerks from Jen Vnam. It was this August Shika who laid out the commune and carried out works on the site of the said image, in particular erecting the temple, the enclosing wall, and the pinnacled temple. The August Shika carried out this project on behalf of Vamashiva. The latter advised His Majesty to incorporate Bhavalaya commune [the family's property] as well as Rha commune, Ryyen commune and Nagasundara into Bhadrapattana, and this was so recorded in an edict.

The August Hiranyaruci, a younger brother of Vamashiva and known as the August priest of Vnam Kansa, was also serving as dean of spiritual preceptors at the court of His Majesty Paramashivaloka. He too petitioned the sovereign for land in Stuk Ransi in the territory of Amoghapura, where he founded the commune of Stuk Ransi and chose a suitable place for setting up an image. Vamashiva and this Hiranyaruci next brought three nieces born of the same mother from Kuti commune in the territory of Purvadisa and settled two of them in Stuk Ransi and one in Bhadrapattana. Other members of the family not so brought continued to live in Kuti commune. These people were the progenitors of the lines in Kuti commune, in Bhadrapattana, and in Stuk Ransi. Their descendants, never sharing their inheritance, were officiants before the Sovereign High Lord of the World. Some served as deans of spiritual preceptors while others served as instructors of sacrifice, officiating in the holy Court of Sacrifices. They remained members of the royal service, and administered the family's estate. Successive members of the line included spiritual preceptors in all grades of the royal government from that time on.

During the reigns of Their Majesties Rudraloka [Harshavarman I] and Paramarudraloka [Ishanavarman II], various members of the family continued to officiate before the Sovereign High Lord of the World as before. The August Kumarashvamin, a nephew of Vamashiva, served as dean of spiritual preceptors and was family head. He founded the commune of Parashara on land belonging to Stuk Ransi, and managed an endowment which Their Majesties placed under the family's authority.

The capital is moved to Chok Gargyar, today known as Koh Ker. Members of the priestly family relocate as well and acquire land in the area.

During the reign of His Majesty Paramashivapada [Jayavarman IV], when the sovereign left the royal city of Sri Yashodharapura to reign in Chok Gargyar, he took the Sovereign High Lord of the World with him. Members of the family continued to officiate before the divinity as before. The August Ishanamurti, a grandson of Vamashiva, served as dean of spiritual preceptors, was family head, and took up residence in Chok Gargyar. He sued for land in Chok Gargyar, laid out the commune of Khmvan, and assigned slaves to it. He gave an endowment to the sanctuary at Chok Gargyar, which was under the family's authority. It was this Ishanamurti who set up the holy linga in Stuk Ransi.

During the reign of His Majesty Brahmaloka [King Harshavarman II], members of the family continued to officiate before the Sovereign High Lord of the World as before. The August Atmashiva, a nephew of Ishanamurti, who had been chaplain to the Sovereign High Lord of the World, served as instructor in sacrifice and was family head.

King Rajendravarman moves the capital back to the Angkor area.

When His Majesty Shivaloka [King Rajendravarman]) returned to reign in the royal city of Yashodharapura, he brought the Sovereign High Lord of the World back with him. Members of the family continued to officiate before that divinity as before. The said Atmashiva was chaplain to the Sovereign High Lord of the World, served as instructor of sacrifice, and was family head. He built the temple and pinnacle at Stuk Ransi, founded Brahmapura commune, the settlement of Katuka and the settlement of Santi, all on land belonging to Stuk Ransi, and set up images in them. He died in the time of His Majesty Paramaviraloka [King Jayavarman V].

In the following section, Sadashiva alludes to civil unrest, desecration and the apparently forced vacating of property. He gives no explanation, simply stating it as fact. As in many things, Old Khmer passages are often more frank and practical than Sanskrit ones, which contain no mention of violence.

During the reign of His Majesty Paramaviraloka, members of the family continued to officiate before the Sovereign High Lord of the World as before. The August Shivacarya, a grandson of Atmashiva, was chaplain to the Sovereign High Lord of the World and family head. After His Majesty Nirvanapada [King Suryavarman I], only two years on the throne, had sent troops out against those who had desecrated the images in Bhadrapattana and Stuk Ransi, this Shivacarya restored those images, which were family property. In Bhadrapattana commune he set up an image of Shankaranarayana and an image of Bhagavati, not family property, and gave them slaves. He died before he could finish rebuilding the commune and various deserted settlements.

Sadashiva takes over reconstruction tasks that his late uncle had begun. The historian priest is given another promotion, to the rank of *kamsten*, with the name Jayendrapandita, which might be rendered as Victorious-Shiva-wiseman.

During the reign of His Majesty Nirvanapada, members of the family continued to officiate before the Sovereign High Lord of the World as before. The August Sadashiva, a nephew of Shivacarya, was chaplain to the Sovereign High Lord of the World, and was family head. His Majesty bade him retire from holy orders so that he might give him to wife a younger sister of the chief queen My High Lady Sri Viralakshmi. His Majesty named him Kamsten Sri Jayendrapandita and made him royal chaplain as well as director first-class of the Karmantara order.

When Bhadrapattana commune, Stuk Ransi commune and their [outlying] settlements were abandoned when His Majesty Nirvanapada sent out his troops, it was this Sri Jayendrapandita who rebuilt the said commune and consecrated their images, which he had restored. In Bhadrapattana commune he set up a holy linga and two images not family property, gave them all manner of costly things, and gave them slaves. He built a pinnacled temple and an enclosing laterite wall, made fields and gardens, dug a reservoir, and built a dam. In Bhadravasa commune he consecrated its image, gave it all manner of costly things, made fields and gardens, dug a reservoir, and built a dam. In Bhadragiri commune he consecrated its image, laid out the commune again, built a dam, an enclosing wall and a stable for all of the cows belonging to the divinity. In Stuk Ransi commune he consecrated its image, gave it all manner of costly things, dug a moat, made gardens, dug a reservoir, and built a dam.

This same Sri Jayendrapandita petitioned His Majesty Nirvanapada for the grant of a piece of land in Amoghapura called Camka, a hundred vroh in extent. He purchased another tract, 30 vroh in extent, east of the sanctuary of Travan Maharatha in exchange for one vessel, one cuspidor, and cloth for lower garments. He bought yet another tract, 60 vroh in extent, on the river Amoghapura called Pralak Kvan Ne, in exchange for two vessels, two cuspidors, and cloth for lower garments. He and his family gave these several tracts to the sanctuary in Stuk Ransi.

Sri Jayendrapandita also founded a settlement in Amoghapura on a piece of land called Nagasundara, which had been family property; he assigned slaves and paddy to it, and gave it to the sanctuary at Bhadrapattana. His Majesty Nirvanapada had him acquire certain ricelands in Ganeshvara to give to the clerical staff, the sovereign directing him to give some riceland in Vrac in payment. Boundary markers were set up which divided the riceland at Bhadrapattana with the sanctuary at Stuk Ransi.

In Brahmapura commune he set up an image of Bhagavati, gave it slaves, made a garden, dug a reservoir, and built a dam. In the territory of Purvadisha, in the former commune of Kuti, he laid out that abandoned commune again and rebuilt the entire enclosing wall there. He set up a holy linga one cubit high, built a temple, gave it slaves and all manner of costly things.

Having petitioned His Majesty Paramanirvanapada for the grant of a tract of ravaged land in Bahuyuddha in the commune of Jen Dnap, he set up markers of the metes and bounds on it and, together with members of his family, gave it to the sanctuary at Kuti.

Now come more references to unrest.

> The commune of Bhavalaya had been given to the family by the High Lord Shivakaivalya, who founded it in the vicinity of Amarendrapura. As stated in the edict in Bhadrapattana, it had been pillaged and was deserted, the commune itself and the holy linga reverting to wilderness thereafter along with the sanctuary. Later, Sri Jayendrapandita, having advised His Majesty Sri Udayadityavarman that this commune Bhavalaya belonged to his line, the sovereign returned it to the family, and he [Jayendrapandita] cleared it of wild growth, consecrated its image, and resumed worship. He was instructed to ascertain the whereabouts of the sanctuary's slaves who had been driven out, resettle them in the commune, return them to the divinity, and re-establish Bhavalaya as a commune belonging as before to Bhadrapattana.

> Being a kinsman on his father's side of the Dust of the Feet Sri Vagindrapandita of Siddhayatana commune in Purvadisa, Sri Jayendrapandita was the one who performed the obsequies for him. It was he [Vagindrapandita] who had founded the said commune, set up its image, and inaugurated its reservoir. Sri Jayendrapandita built the ashram [there], assigned slaves to it, and gave it to Vagindrapandita's sanctuary as a [final] gift to a guru.

Sadashiva is honoured with the Dust of the Feet title, possibly in connection with an assignment to be tutor to the future king Udayadityavarman II.

> While His Majesty Sri Udayadityavarman was on the throne, various members of the family continued to officiate before the Sovereign High Lord of the World as before. As royal preceptor, Sri Jayendrapandita was now given a new title, Dust of the Feet My Holy High Lord Sri Jayendravarman. [Under his tutelage] Sri Udayadityavarman studied various branches of learning, in particular science, grammar, jurisprudence, and other subjects. His Majesty celebrated his royal initiatory rites, notably the Bhuvanadhva and the holy Brahmayajna, and performed a great festival according to the holy Secret Doctrine.

> [On Sri Jayendravarman] he bestowed gifts of respect to a guru and costly things, notably such accessories as diadems, earrings, armlets, bracelets, a magnificent head ornament, a royal seat of silver, a golden ewer, a fly-whisk, and a three-headed palanquin.

> *These were given to him for his [personal] use. The sovereign [also] bestowed on him jewels, gold, silver, and all manner of costly things: a thousand sacred cows, two hundred elephants, a hundred and one horses, and a hundred rams and buffaloes, and a thousand male and female slaves. [In addition,] he gave him three communes: two on Samkaraparvata and one, Mano commune, in Jen Taran. My High Lord and Master Sri Udayadityavarman kept him in the royal city and did constant honor to him. He had him write down the names of individuals in daily service together with requisites for service such as habits, victuals, drink, condiments, and areca nuts – all these being needed for service to the Sovereign High Lord of the World which Sri Jayendravarman made use of daily.*

> *His Majesty gave the ravaged commune of Stuk Rmman to Sri Jayendravarman for his maintenance, together with Stuk Ransi commune. When Sri Jayendravarman expressed a desire to set up an image, His Majesty gave him a holy linga two cubits in height and various costly things as objects of use for the said image and various costly things by way of gifts of respect to a guru [to Sri Jayendravarman].*

Sadashiva again describes the construction of his family's temple, noting the king's close involvement in the project.

> *His Majesty ordered a minister to go and lay out the commune named Bhadraniketana on land in Bhadrapattana belonging to the new Dust of the Feet My Holy High Lord Sri Jayendravarman, to set up on his behalf a holy linga two cubits in height, and to give four hundred male and female slaves to the image. Sri Jayendravarman [thereafter] erected a stone temple with pinnacle, dug a reservoir, built dikes, and laid out fields and gardens.*

Now begins another lengthy description of the acquisition of land. With something as important as land as the subject, the inscription gives its first dates, based on the Hindu Shaka calendar.

The titles 'Chlon' and 'Lon' appear frequently in this section. Their meaning and place in the hierarchy of the time are not well understood, so they are not translated here. The title 'Vap' appears to signify a low-ranking official.

The year Shaka 974, in which Sadashiva set up the *linga* at his temple, is commonly taken among historians as the date of the temple's consecration, 1052 AD, but by other experts' calculations corresponds to 1053.

The Sdok Kok Thom Inscription

The following section gives origins of the settlement Anrem Lon, and how it came to belong to Sadashiva's clan. Great texts always contain a few typos. In the first sentence below, the Brahmin son Madhava is called first by the title *'Chlon'*. In the next sentence his title is given as *'Lon'*, but it returns to *'Chlon'* in later references.

During the reign of His Majesty Paramaviraloka [Jayavarman V], the Brahmin Samkarsha and his son the Chlon *Madhava, foreigners both, had purchased land on which to lay out the settlement of Anrem Lon. Assigning slaves to it, they set up a holy Shivalinga as property of the* Lon *Madhava. The lord Chlon Samkarsha died in the reign of His Majesty Paramaviraloka, survived by his son the* Chlon *Madhava. In Shaka 965, with the reign of His Majesty Paramanirvanapada, the* Chlon *Madhava submitted a petition to His Majesty requesting him to grant title to the said settlement of Anrem Lon and its slaves to Sri Jayendravarman. The slaves of this service were kept until Shaka 967. The* Chlon *Madhava died in Shaka 971 while Sri Udayadityavarman was still on the throne.*

In Shaka 974 Sri Jayendravarman set up a Shivalinga as High Lord of the World in Bhadraniketana. A communication was addressed to His Majesty requesting him to permit the said settlement of Anrem Lon and its slaves to be another royal benefice to the High Lord of the World in the Shivalinga at Bhadraniketana. His Majesty gave him title to the said settlement and its slaves, just as he had done previously at the desire of the Chlon *Madhava, who received the same support. Sri Jayendravarman dedicated that settlement and its slaves to the service of the High Lord of the World in the Shivalinga at Bhadraniketana.*

The origin of the settlement of Anrem Lon: In Shaka 894, on the third day, Wednesday, of the first fortnight of Pushya, the Brahmin the lord Chlon *Samkarsha and his son the* Chlon *Madhava, foreigners both, had bought a tract of land from residents of Anrem Lon belonging to the Karmantara order, namely the* Lon *Para, the* Lon *Dharmapala, the* Lon *Go, the* Lon *Sarvajna, the Venerable Shivapada, the military commander, and the governor of the territory of Khdak. Given in exchange for the purchase were 2 taels of gold, 320 lower garments, 1 yau of thnap cloth, 4 goats, 4 sacred cows, and 12 water buffaloes. Metes and bounds of the land in the settlement, together with riceland to the north: on the east it abuts on land of Dhanavaha; on the south it extends to Dnan; on the west it extends to the oxcart road west of Snval; on the north it runs to the paddy-burning ground, turns and reaches back to the bank of the reservoir; on the east again it extends to the sacred margosa tree, then abuts on land belonging to Thpvan Rmman.*

Land also part of the settlement of Anrem Lon: in Shaka 901, on the third day of the fortnight of the waxing moon of Pushya, the Brahmin named the lord Chlon Samkarsha and the Chlon Madhava purchased a tract from sellers vap Ishvaravindu, Vap Ajya, and Vap Bhima. Given in exchange were 2 taels of gold, 5 vessels for liquids, 5 flasks, 5 yau of stitched cloth, and 300 lower garments. Metes and bounds of the said land: on the east it abuts on land belonging to the sanctuary at Thpvan Rmman; on the south it abuts on land belonging to Anrem Lon; on the west it follows the boundary markers; on the north it again follows the boundary markers; on the west again it follows the high forest.

A tract on the share inherited by the Venerable Mat of Gnan commune was acquired both from the cleric Sralen Vay Nuk of Cun Chdin, a member of their family, and from an individual with him named the Lon Yak Ral, the area all told being 40 vroh. This land formed part of the settlement of Anrem Lon, the residence of the Chlon Madhava.

With the lands of Anrem Lon thoroughly defined, Sadashiva now turns to its slaves. It is in texts like this that some of the names of society's lowest-ranking members have been immortalised. It is unclear why almost all the slaves mentioned are elderly women.

Slaves assigned to the settlement of Anrem Lon by the lord Chlon Samkarsha and the Chlon Madhava for the purpose of giving them to the sanctuary: to the western sector were assigned the male Thpvan Tyak and the elderly female E from Shivapada Danden; to the central sector of the commune was assigned the elderly female Thlem from the commune of Vrai Guya in the district of Purvadisha; also to the central sector of the commune was assigned the elderly female Khdep, likewise from the commune of [Vrai] Guya in the district of Purvadisha; also to the central sector of the commune were assigned the male Mat of Gnan commune and the elderly female Ja from Samtac Dray in the territory of Karom; to the eastern sector was assigned the elderly female Kamyan from Lingapura; also to the eastern sector were assigned the male Tem Khvit and the elderly female Srashta, residents of Anrem Lon, who were taken in exchange for other slaves; also to the western sector was assigned a kinswoman of the male Thpvan Tyak, namely the elderly female Rudrani from Shresthapura.

Khmer architecture conveys a love of straight lines and geometry. In the following section, Sadashiva documents the new temple's land holdings by describing eight azimuths radiating out in the four cardinal and four intermediate directions. The Khmers of course did not know the metric system. Sak-Humphry arrived at the measurements given in metres through some typical deduction of the Khmer historian's trade. The text gives numbers of distance units without specifying the unit, implying that it was in common use. Sak-Humphry posits that it was probably a unit known as the *'hat'*, mentioned on other stones and likely similar to an Indian unit, the *'hasta'* or cubit of about 45 centimetres.

It is unclear whether any of the adjacent Thai villages of modern times existed in those days and appear in this text under Old Khmer names.

The new commune of Bhadraniketana stands on land belonging to Bhadrapattana, and to the east of land belonging to the new Bhadrapattana. On the southeast it extends to the boundary markers of Stuk Kadamba, abutting on land belonging to Len Tvar commune, a distance of about 216 metres; on the south it runs as far as Srau Sramoc, again abutting on land belonging to Len Tvar commune, a distance of about 149 metres; on the southwest it extends to the boundary markers of Kupa, [still] abutting on land of Len Tvar, a distance of about 234 metres; on the west it runs as far as Stuk Tannot, abutting on land belonging to Gnan commune, a distance of about 1.1 kilometres; on the northwest it extends to the boundary-markers of Lmun commune, abutting on land belonging to the commune and settlement of Ten Tvan and the river Gargyar, a distance of about 1.2 kilometres; on the north it extends to Stuk Run, abutting on land belonging to Cvar Mo commune, a distance of about 738 metres; on the northeast, finally, lies land belonging to Bhadrapattana.

Now comes an equally detailed documentation of the Gnan commune, given by the king to support the temple.

As a royal offering, His Majesty My High Lord Sri Udayaditya-varman gave to the said holy linga at Bhadraniketana the commune named Gnan of Cranan Vo and its inhabitants with 151 households, as well as the land of that sector. Metes and bounds of the said land in Gnan commune of Cranan Vo: on the east it runs to Stuk Tannot, abutting on land belonging to the new commune of Bhadraniketana, a distance of about 608 metres; on the southeast it extends to the boundary markers on land belonging to Len Tvar commune, a distance of about 896 metres; on the south it extends to the boundary markers on land belonging to the commune of Vrai Ramvan Candraya, a distance of about 472.5 metres; on the southwest it runs as far as the boundary markers on land belonging to the commune of Shivapattana of the Sramo Em, a distance of about 720 metres; on the west it extends to the boundary markers of land belonging to Anlan commune, a distance of about 716 metres; on the northwest it extends to the boundary markers on land belonging to Vajravarman commune, a distance of about 1.2 kilometres; on the north it extends to the boundary markers north of Mount Vren, abutting on land belonging to Jhe Rlom commune and Tvan Mvay Tem commune, a distance of about 2.9 kilometres; on the northeast it runs as far as the boundary markers abutting on land belonging to the commune of Chdin Gargyar, a distance of about 945 metres.

Finally, the space on the stone nearly exhausted, the priest gives a list of the labour teams that will serve the new temple on waning moon/waxing moon shifts. Nearby ashrams are also mentioned.

Slaves of My Holy High Lord in the Shivalinga at Bhadraniketana, royal offerings: Gnan commune: First fortnight, 2 male overseers and their party of 27 males and 48 females. Second fortnight, 2 male overseers and their party of 27 males and 45 females. Total, males and females: 151.

Slaves of the High Lord of the World of the Shivalinga at Bhadraniketana. Gnan commune: First fortnight of service: 1 male overseer and his party of 21 males and 54 females. Second fortnight: 1 male foreman, 2 male warders, and their party of 15 males and 50 females. Ashram south of the causeway near the moat: 1 male overseer and his party of 4 males and 11 females; Ashram near the wall: 1 male overseer and his party of 7 males and 13 females; Ashram south of the sanctuary: 1 male overseer and his party of 4 males and 16 females.

Settlement of Anrem Lon: 1 male overseer and his party of 46 males and 54 females; First fortnight of service: 1 male overseer and his party of 20 males and 53 females. [Second fortnight]: 1 male foreman, 2 male warders, and their party of 21 males and 43 females; Ashram north of the causeway: 1 male overseer and his party of 4 males and 10 females; Ashram north of the sanctuary: 1 male overseer and his party of 8 males and 20 females; The other ashram north of the sanctuary: 1 male overseer and his party of 4 males and 13 females.

Settlement of Pin Khla: 1 male overseer and his party of 4 males and 13 females.

With those details about the labour team of Pin Khla, Sadashiva completes his lengthy *cri de coeur*. A stone carver gets to work. Erected in the northeast corner of Sdok Kok Thom's gallery, protected from the elements, the resulting stele survives more than eight centuries to take its place in modern times as the most important written record left by the Khmer civilisation. Let us be grateful that the Brahmin chose to tell us of a founder-king who conducted an historic rite atop a mountain, a father and son, foreigners both, who bought a parcel of land, an elderly slave woman named Srashta who arrived to live in a rural hamlet. Without these stories in stone, our view into the Khmer past would be far less clear than it is.

Glossary

Anastylosis: A method of reconstruction of historic buildings in which recovered elements such as fallen stones are returned to their former places in an effort to restore original appearance and form.

Angkor: The Khmer Empire's main capital, located near modern day Siem Reap.

Angkor Wat: The largest of the temples of Angkor, built in the 12th century by King Suryavarman II.

Aranyaprathet: The Thai border town that lies about 30 kilometres southwest of Sdok Kok Thom.

Baphuon: State temple of King Udayadityavarman II, built mid-11th century.

baray: A holy reservoir, generally rectangular and built to the east of a temple. Most historians call *barays* symbolic representations of the Hindu Sea of Creation. There is disagreement as to whether they also functioned as holding tanks for irrigation waters.

Bayon: The great sculpted temple at the centre of Angkor Thom city. Due to a misreading of the Sdok Kok Thom inscription, the Bayon was long mistakenly dated as being built in about 900 AD, almost three centuries before its actual construction.

Beng Mealea: The 12th century temple complex that lies about forty kilometres east of Angkor and was once mistakenly thought to be the work of Jayavarman II, the empire's founder.

Black Buddha: A life-size sitting image formerly located outside the inner *gopura* of Sdok Kok Thom. Cambodian refugees took the image to be a Buddha; it is actually an image of a Thai monk, Luang Poh Boon Tham, who had lived at the temple prior to the refugee exodus.

Brahma: One of the Hindu trinity, 'the Creator.' Brahma was rarely represented in Khmer art, though some temples had towers devoted to him.

Brahman: The Hindu Godhead, the unknowable, formless cosmic essence of which all Hindu gods are but manifestations.

Brahmins: The religious elite of the Khmer Empire. These Hindu priests functioned as advisors to kings, tenders of *lingas* and lords of large rice-producing estates.

Camp 007: The huge refugee camp that sprang up around Sdok Kok Thom in 1979. It was later known as Camp Rithisen, after a character in Khmer mythology.

Champa: An ancient Hindu state located in what is today southern Vietnam. Champa and its dominant ethnic group, the Chams, were rivals to the Khmers.

Chao Poh Sisuto: The great resident spirit of Sdok Kok Thom, under the name known to local Thais.

Chenla: The Khmer Empire's predecessor state, possibly in fact a collection of independent principalities.

Glossary

Damrong, H.R.H. Prince Rajanupab: Thai scholar-prince who in the late 19th and early 20th centuries founded Thailand's modern education system, conducted historical research and established programs to study and safeguard antiquities.

Dangrek Mountain Range: Mountains that run east-west and form a border between Cambodia's north and Thailand's Isaan region.

Darshana: A Hindu concept of worship and prayer in which communication flows both ways between a human being and a god.

devaraja: In Sanskrit, literally god-king. This term, found in the Sdok Kok Thom inscription, sparked a still unresolved debate over religious practice in the Khmer court.

L'École française d'Extrême-Orient: The French School of Asian Studies, primary French academic institution concerning subjects Khmer, founded in 1900. Its academic journal, *Le Bulletin d'École française d'Extrême-Orient*, published many of the early French examinations of ancient Khmer subjects.

estampage: French term for a high-quality rubbing of an inscription or bas relief.

Fine Arts Department: The Thai government body that oversees antiquities in Thailand.

Funan: The first known Hindu state in Southeast Asia, believed to have come into being in the Mekong River Delta around the 3rd century AD.

Garuda: The Bird God. Enemy of the *naga*, the mount of Vishnu.

gopura: A temple gate, often an elaborate architectural statement. Typically the eastern *gopura* is the largest, helping create an eastern orientation for the temple as a whole.

Hariharalaya: The Khmer Empire's first long-term capital, known today as the Roluos area about twelve kilometres east of Siem Reap.

Jayavarman II: Founder of the Khmer Empire. Through conquest and cajoling, he knit a collection of feuding principalities into the first Khmer state. Crowned atop Mount Mahendra north of Angkor, he later ruled from the city of Hariharalaya, today known as Roluos. Reigned c. 800-830.

Jayavarman VII: One of the greatest kings of the Khmer Empire. He drove out Cham occupiers and oversaw a building program that created Angkor Thom city, the Bayon and numerous other temples. Reigned 1181 – c. 1218.

Khmer People's National Liberation Front: The political organisation that unified feuding Khmer Serei factions to fight the Vietnamese in the war that began with the overthrow of the Khmer Rouge in 1979.

Khmer Serei: The 'Free Khmer', anti-communist Cambodian resistance groups that fought against the Vietnamese occupation – and often against each other – following the 1979 downfall of the Khmer Rouge.

Khmer Rouge: The fanatical movement that took power in Cambodia in 1975, emptying the cities and turning the country into a huge forced labour camp. Millions of Cambodians died of starvation and disease and in purges during the rule of the Khmer Rouge, who were overthrown by a Vietnamese invasion force in 1979.

Koke Soong: The Thai administrative district in which Sdok Kok Thom stands; also the name of a major village in the district.

Kulen: The hills that stand to the north of Angkor and provided much of its sandstone.

laterite: The thick soil material typically used in bases, foundations, walls, landings and other utilitarian elements of Khmer architecture. Laterite is cut easily from the ground and hardens on exposure to the air.

library: A smallish building typically found with a twin on either side of a Khmer temple's processional walkway. Early French scholars believed that the structures were repositories for sacred texts, hence the name, but other theories say that they served as ancillary chapels to their temple's main sanctuary.

linga: The symbol, generally a stone shaft, of the god Shiva. Religious life at Khmer temples typically revolved around tending of its *lingas*.

lintel: The upper horizontal element of a door frame. In Khmer buildings, these are often elaborately carved and thus of special interest to art collectors and thieves.

mandala: A complex circular diagram-design of great spiritual significance in the Hindu-Buddhist tradition, representing the cosmos at large and the human role in it.

Muang Boran: The Ancient City, a huge historical theme park outside Bangkok that includes a replica of Sdok Kok Thom's inner courtyard, built at roughly half scale.

naga: A magical serpent, often with multiple heads. *Nagas* are generally benevolent figures in Khmer spirituality – the daughter of the King of the *Nagas* is held to be the mother of the Khmer race. Stone *nagas* are common elements at Khmer temples.

Nong Samet: The Thai village that lies closest to Sdok Kok Thom.

Norodom: Cambodian king who in 1863 signed the agreement that made his realm a French protectorate. Reigned 1860-1904.

Old Khmer: The Khmer Empire's vernacular language, a forebear of modern Cambodian.

Phimai: The largest of the Khmer-era temples in Thailand, located in Nakhon Ratchasima province. Built mainly in the late 11th to late 12th centuries, the temple was dedicated to the Buddha.

Phnom Bakheng: The hilltop temple just northwest of Angkor Wat. Phnom Bakheng was the state temple of King Yasovarman after he moved the capital from Hariharalaya.

Phnom Rung: Khmer temple in Thailand's Buriram province. Built from the early 10th to the late 12th century, its primary material is pinkish sandstone.

Glossary

prasat: A stone temple, often with a central tower.

Pre Rup: The state temple of King Rajendravarman II in Angkor. Topped by five towers, it has a red hue due to its primary materials laterite and brick. Built in the mid-10th century.

Preah Vihear: A Khmer temple that stands atop a cliff in the Dangrek mountain range. Built from the late 9th to the mid-12th centuries, it has a rare north-south, linear layout. The World Court ruled in 1962 that the temple lies in Cambodia, but ownership remains a source of tension with Thailand.

Rajendravarman II: Khmer king who returned the capital from Koh Ker to the Angkor region and established greater central control in the empire's system of government. Reigned c. 944-c. 968.

Sadashiva: Abbot of Sdok Kok Thom in the mid-11th century, presumed author of the Sdok Kok Thom inscription.

Sakaew: Thai border province in which Sdok Kok Thom is located.

sandstone: The high-quality material of Khmer temples. Much of Angkor's sandstone was quarried in the Kulen hills.

Sanskrit: The ancient Indian tongue that was the language of religion, art and state affairs in the Khmer Empire. Sanskrit deeply influenced the modern languages of Cambodia, Thailand and Laos.

Shiva: One of the trinity of Hindu gods, 'the Destroyer.' Shiva was the god of most Khmer kings, sharing many royal attributes, among them great power, war-making abilities and a tendency not to mingle with ordinary human beings.

Sihanouk: Cambodian royal who led his country through much of its tumultuous post-independence era as prince, king and politician. Overthrown in 1970, he aligned himself with Cambodian communists, but later split with them. He was restored as king in 1993 and abdicated in 2004.

stele: Free-standing object on which an inscription is carved

Suryavarman I: Khmer king who fought his way to the throne and had one of the empire's longest reigns, c. 1002-1050.

Suryavarman II: Khmer king who built Angkor Wat. After taking power in a series of coups, he tied the empire more closely together and waged wars against the Chams and Annamites. Reigned 1113-c. 1150.

Udayadityavarman II: Khmer king during the time Sadashiva authored the Sdok Kok Thom inscription. Builder of the Baphuon temple in Angkor. Reigned 1050-c. 1066.

Vishnu: One of the trinity of Hindu gods, 'the Preserver.' Vishnu intervenes frequently in human affairs through incarnations, the most prominent of whom are Rama, hero of the *Ramayana* epic, and Krishna.

Further Reading

Michael D. Coe, 2003. *Angkor and the Khmer Civilization*, New York, Thames & Hudson.

Charles Higham, 2001. *The Civilization of Angkor*, Los Angeles and Berkeley, University of California Press.

Claude Jacques and Micheal Freeman, 2006. *Ancient Angkor*, Bangkok, River Books. This is a detailed and essential guide to Angkor.

Claude Jacques and Michael Freeman, 2007. *Angkor – Cities and Temples*, Bangkok, River Books.

Claude Jacques and Philippe Lafond, 2007. *The Khmer Empire: Cities and Sanctuaries from the 5th to the 13th Century*, Bangkok, River Books.

Ian Mabbett and David Chandler, 1995. *The Khmers*, Oxford, UK and Cambridge, Mass. Blackwell Publishers.

All of the above books provide solid introductions to Khmer history and culture.

Étienne Aymonier, 1900-1904. *Le Cambodge*, Paris, Ernest Leroux, Éditeur. This seminal work of Aymonier can be found in specialist libraries and is online in its entirety. Volume II was translated into English by Walter E.J. Tips and published as two books, *Khmer Heritage in Thailand* and *Khmer Heritage in the Old Siamese Provinces of Cambodia*, by White Lotus Press in 1999.

Kamaleswar Bhattacharya in collaboration with Karl-Heinz Golzio, 2009. *A Selection of Sanskrit Inscriptions from Cambodia*, Center for Khmer Studies. This includes the Sanskrit portion of the Sdok Kok Thom inscription.

Adhir Chakravarti, 1978. *The Sdok Kak Thom Inscription*, Calcutta, Sanskrit College Calcutta. This two-volume work includes an English translation and historical commentary.

Chhany Sak-Humphry with the assistance of Philip N. Jenner, 2005. *The Sdok Kak Thom Inscription*, Phnom Penh, The Buddhist Institute. This is Sak-Humphry's original translation, with commentary that focuses on questions of Old Khmer grammar.

Many editions of 19th century French academic journals such as *Journal Asiatique* and the *Bulletin de l'École française d'Extrême-Orient*, in which pioneering writings on Khmer history appeared, can be easily found at French websites through use of search engines.

Joyce Clark (editor), 2007 *Bayon: New Perspectives*, Bangkok, River Books. An up to date account of new and at times competing interpretations of the Bayon Temple.

Zhou Daguan, translated by Peter Harris, 2007. *A Record of Cambodia: The Land and its*

People, Chiang Mai, Silkworm Books. This is the full text of the writings of Zhou, the Chinese envoy who visited Angkor in 1296 and is quoted in almost every book about the Khmer Empire.

Piere Dieulefils, texts by Louis Finot and Lunet de la Jonquière, 2006. *Ruins of Angkor: Cambodia in 1909*, Bangkok, River Books. This book contains magnificent photographs of Angkor as it was over a century ago.

Henri Mouhot, 1966. *Henri Mouhot's Diary: Travels in Central Parts of Siam, Cambodia and Laos during the Years 1858-61*, Oxford, Oxford University Press. This classic of Khmer history literature, translated into English and reissued, recounts Mouhot's travels in his own words.

Vittorio Roveda, with photographs by Jaro Poncar, 2003. *Sacred Angkor: The Carved Reliefs of Angkor Wat*, Bangkok, River Books. Using scenes from the great bas reliefs, this book delves deep into Khmer mythology.

Milton Osborne, 1975. *River Road to China: The Mekong River Expedition, 1866-73*, New York, Liveright. This recounts early French colonial relations in Cambodia and the failed effort to find an easily navigable route into China up the Mekong.

William Shawcross, 1984. *The Quality of Mercy: Cambodia, Holocaust and Modern Conscience*, New York, Simon & Schuster, 1984.

Linda Mason and Roger Brown, 1983. *Rice, Rivalry, and Politics: Managing Cambodian Relief*, University of Notre Dame Press.

The above two books recount the Cambodian refugee crisis that began in 1979 and the outside world's response to it.

Elizabeth Becker, 1998. *When the War Was Over: Cambodia and the Khmer Rouge Revolution*, New York, PublicAffairs revised edition. An account of the modern history of Cambodia and the Khmer Rouge.